John Cleary

***

Bilanzen und Steuern der Limited in Deutschland

Bibliographische Information:
Die Deutsche Bibliothek verzeichnet diesen Titel in der Deutschen Nationalbibliografie. Bibliografische Daten sind unter http://dnb.ddb.de verfügbar.

John Cleary

Bilanzen und Steuern der Limited in Deutschland

Reihe: Die Limited in Deutschland (Band 2)

1. Auflage 2006

ISBN 10:3-937686-27-4

ISBN 13: 978-3937686-27-1

Nachdruck, auch auszugsweise, nur mit schriftlicher Genehmigung des Verlags

© CT Salzwasser-Verlag GmbH & Co. KG, Bremen, 2006 (www.salzwasserverlag.de)

Druck und Herstellung: Hohnholt Reprografischer Betrieb GmbH, Bremen (www.hohnholt.com)

Dieser Titel unterliegt dem Gesetz zur Regelung der Preisbindung von Verlagserzeugnissen (BGBl. I Nr. 63 vom 5. September 2002)

Inhaltsverzeichnis

Einführung	**6**
Englische Gesellschaften im Ausland	6
Allgemeines zur Rechnungslegung in England	7
Arten von Unternehmen in England	8
Grundzüge der Rechnungslegung	**9**
Regularien und ihre Überwachung	11
Gesetzliche Regeln	13
Regelungen der Berufsverbände	15
Regeln der Wertpapierbörse	16
Regeln des IASC	17
Andere Einflüsse	17
Bilanzierungsrichtlinien	**20**
Das Prinzip getrennter Unternehmenseinheiten	21
Bewertung in Geld	21
Dauerhaftigkeit des Unternehmens	22
Anschaffungskosten statt Zeitwert	22
Gewinnbilanzierung bei Realisierung	23
Verlustbilanzierung bei Entstehung	23
Verteilung von Aufwendungen auf Bilanzperioden	23
Einheitlichkeit der Bilanz	24
Prinzip der konservativen Bilanzierung	25
Nur wesentliche Informationen	25
Formvorschriften	**27**
Zwingende Form	27
Jahresberichte	28
Die Einnahme-Überschussrechnung	**29**
Zulässige Muster	29
Einzelpositionen in den Mustern	32
Die Handelsbilanz	**54**
Zur Verfügung stehende Muster	54
Allgemeine Bewertungsgrundsätze	55
Current Cost Accounting	56
Neubewertung von Vermögenswerten	57
Inhalt der Bilanz	58
Anlagevermögen (fixed assets)	58
Immaterielle Vermögenswerte (intangible assets)	59
Sachanlagen (tangible assets)	61

Gemietete Vermögensgegenstände (Leased assets)	62
Investitionen (Investments)	64
Umlaufvermögen (Current Assets)	65
Forderungen (Deptors)	66
Kassenbestand und Bankkonto	67
Verbindlichkeiten (Creditors)	67
Rückstellungen für Gewährleistung und Verbindlichkeiten	69
Kapital und Reserven	69
Sonstige Reserven	70
Interessen von Minderheitsbeteiligten	70
Eventualverbindlichkeiten und Verpflichtungen	71
Ereignisse nach Bilanzerstellung	72
Cash flow statement	73
Andere Erklärungen und Berichte	73
Erklärung über die gesamten Gewinne und Verluste	73
Erklärung über Veränderungen bei der Bilanzierung	74
Bericht des Geschäftsführers	74
Bericht des Wirtschaftsprüfers	75
Anlagen und Muster	**77**
Einnahme-Überschuss-Rechnung: Zugelassene Formate	77
Muster 1	77
Muster 2	78
Muster 3	79
Muster 4	80
Bilanz: Zugelassene Formate	81
Muster 1	81
Muster 2	82
Mustersatzung	82
Mustersatzung	83
Auszüge aus dem Companies Act	87
Anhang 1 zum Companies Act (Form and Content of Company Accounts)	155

EINFÜHRUNG

Englische Gesellschaften im Ausland

Englische juristische Personen - allen voran die Limited - können seit einigen Jahren ohne weiteres Ihren Verwaltungssitz ins europäische Ausland verlegen. Dort dürfen sie nach einer Grundsatzentscheidung des Europäischen Gerichtshofes genau wie inländische Gesellschaftsformen - in Deutschland z.B. die GmbH - tätig werden.[1] Dieser Umstand führt dazu, dass solche „Auslands-Limiteds" in ihrem Einsatzland, in diesem Fall also in Deutschland, unbeschränkt steuerpflichtig sind. Hier unterscheiden sie sich nicht von ihren einheimischen Geschwistern. In Deutschland werden beispielsweise bei der Besteuerung einer Limited mit Verwaltungssitz im Inland im Wesentlichen die gleichen Maßstäbe wie bei der Besteuerung einer inländischen GmbH angelegt. Der Inhalt der Bilanzierungs- und Rechnungslegungspflicht nach deutschem Recht unterscheidet sich daher nicht.

Eine wesentliche Besonderheit des Einsatzes einer Limited im Ausland ist jedoch, das auch diese Gesellschaften immer einer strengen, hart sanktionierten Rechnungslegungspflicht in England nachzukommen haben. Diese zusätzliche Hürde für den Betrieb einer Limited im Ausland wird gerne verdrängt, da sie unter Umständen - je nach Art und Umfang des Geschäftsbetriebes der Limited - außerordentlich aufwendig ist. Hinzu kommt, dass sich deutsche Steuerberater oder Rechtsanwälte mit der zugrunde liegenden englischen Rechtsmate-

---

[1] Details bei Degenhardt: Die Limited in Deutschland, 4. Auflage, ISBN 3-937686-43-6

rie nicht auskennen und - mangels Versicherungsschutzes - hier auch nicht verantwortlich tätig werden können. Der Einsatz eines englischen Steuerberaters ist in diesen Fällen also zwingend notwendig, ein Kostenfaktor, den man von vorne herein unbedingt berücksichtigen sollte.[2]

Es gibt jedoch auch einfachere Fälle, etwa die von Mantelgesellschaften oder reinen Holding-Unternehmen, bei denen die Limited kein eigenes operatives Unternehmen betreibt, sondern sich z.B. auf ihre Rolle als persönlich haftende Gesellschafterin einer „Limited & Co KG" beschränkt. In diesen Fällen ist es durchaus möglich, die strikten, aber gut strukturierten und verständlichen Rechnungslegungsvorschriften in England als Unternehmer selber zu erfüllen.

Allgemeines zur Rechnungslegung in England

Viele Personen sind an den Aktivitäten moderner Unternehmen interessiert: Gesellschafter, Investoren, Banken, Geschäftspartner und Behörden. Alle diese Parteien haben das Recht, Informationen über ein Unternehmen zu erhalten, sei es auf gesetzlicher oder vertraglicher Grundlage. Grundlage hierfür ist die Bilanz der Gesellschaft mit all ihren Anhängen, die ihrerseits auf einer gesetzlichern Grundlage basiert. Die zunehmende Reglementierung in diesem Sektor verlangt von den Beteiligten, namentlich den Unternehmern und den Steuerberatern bzw. Buchhaltern des Unternehmens, zunehmende Vertrautheit mit den vielen gesetzlichen Regelungen, deren Nichtbeachtung mannigfaltige Nachteile zur Folge

---

[2] Hierbei ist zu berücksichtigen, dass der Kostenaufwand in England für die Steuerberatung tendenziell höher als in Deutschland ist.

hat. Hinzu kommt, dass in jüngster Zeit immer mehr Unternehmen durch Bilanzskandale - etwa am neuen Markt - aufgefallen sind, was die Schaffung neuer Standards zur Folge hatte, welche die Unternehmen zu befolgen haben.

Arten von Unternehmen in England

Auch wenn im Vereinigten Königreich viele gewerbliche Unternehmungen als Einzelunternehmen geführt werden, kommt doch in der Praxis der „Limited", also der Limited Liability Company, die größter Bedeutung zu. Ihr rechtlicher Status ist weitgehend von der ihrer Gesellschafter entkoppelt und die Haftung der Gesellschafter ist auf ihre Einlage in die Gesellschaft beschränkt. Das gilt auch für die public limited company, die plc (in Wales: „ccc" - cwmni cyfyngedig cyhoeddus), deren weitergehender Sinn unter anderem darin besteht, Streubesitz zuzulassen. Ausschließlich die plc ist es gestattet, an den Kapitalmärkten Geld aufzunehmen und ihre Anteile an der Börse zu platzieren.

Die große Mehrheit der „limited companies" wird jedoch von der „Private Limited" gestellt, also der klassischen „Ltd", deren Erscheinungsbild dadurch geprägt wird, dass sie meist nur eine kleine Anzahl Anteilseigner hat, Anteilsübertragungen nur selten stattfinden und die Anteilseigner oftmals auch einen der Manager des Unternehmens stellen.

GRUNDZÜGE DER RECHNUNGSLEGUNG

Die juristische Trennung von Gesellschaftern und Managern einer Gesellschaft sowie der weitgehende Schutz von Managern einer „Limited" durch das Konzept der Haftungsbeschränkung auf das Gesellschaftsvermögen hat dazu geführt, dass diejenigen Personen in einem Unternehmen, die für dessen Handels- und Finanzaktivitäten verantwortlich sind, umfassend berichtspflichtig sind. Kern dieser Berichtspflicht, die je nach Adressaten (Gesellschafter, Behörden etc.) und abhängig von der Unternehmensgröße unterschiedlich ausgestaltet ist, ist die Bilanz der Limited.

Die Gesellschafter übertragen das Recht und die Pflicht zur Geschäftsführung und damit auch zur ordnungsgemäßen Buchführung von Jahr zu Jahr an das „Board of Directors", also die bestellten Manager des Unternehmens. Bei ihnen verbleiben freilich alle mit der Gesellschafterstellung verbundenen Rechte und Pflichten; dies sind unter Anderem weitgehende Kontrollrechte. Ausgeübt werden diese Kontrollrechte im Wesentlichen in der Gesellschafterversammlung, die bei vielen kleinen „Limiteds" nur aus wenigen Personen bestehen. Von den ca. 1,1 Millionen derzeit existierenden Gesellschaften sind lediglich ca. 3.000 Publikumsgesellschaften mit Streubesitz. Gleichwohl ist auch bei einer kleinen Familiengesellschaft der Geschäftsführer seinen Gesellschaftern verantwortlich.

Der gesamte Komplex der Kontrolle von Gesellschaften kam infolge einiger spektakulärer Unternehmenszusammenbrüche Anfang der 90-er Jahre auf die Tagesordnung und mündete in die Einsatzung des sog. „Cadbury Committee", das sich mit der verbesserten Kontrolle von Unternehmen beschäftigte. Die Untersuchung des Komitees wurde 1992 präsentiert und listete eine Vielzahl von Erfordernissen auf, die zukünftig die Geschäftsführer einer Gesellschaft erfüllen sollten, um dem Bedürfnis nach einer möglichst transparenten, vollständigen und aktuellen Rechnungslegung ihres Unternehmens nachzukommen. Die Geschäftsführer sind danach ihren Gesellschaftern, der Gesellschaft und Dritten gegenüber verpflichtet, vollständige, aussagekräftige und wahre Bilanzen zu erstellen.

Im Allgemeinen wird diesem Erfordernis heute dadurch gerecht geworden, indem die Geschäftsführer für einen bestimmten Zeitraum (zumeist ein Kalenderjahr) über Umsätze und andere Aktivitäten der Firma berichten müssen, bei größeren Unternehmen unterstützt durch halbjährliche Zwischenberichte. Diese Berichte haben die Form von Einnahme-Überschuss-Rechnungen („profit and loss account"; Handelsumsatz, Einnahmen und Ausgaben) und spiegeln den Geldwert aller Geschäftsaktivitäten und ihre Ergebnisse wider, und die Bilanz („the balance sheet"), die die Verhältnisse des Unternehmens zum Geschäftsjahresende und die Einflüsse des vorangegangenen Geschäftsjahres auf die Vermögenswerte und Verbindlichkeiten darstellt.

Begleitet werden diese Dokumente von einem Rückblick des Geschäftsführers („Director") und des Vorsitzenden des Verwaltungsrates („Chief executive") auf wichtige Ereignisse des vergangenen Geschäftsjahres und einer Darstellung der Erwartungen für die nahe Zukunft, die ihrerseits begleitet werden von einem erläuternden Bericht („Qualitative Report") und einer operativen und fiskalischen Bewertung der Unternehmensaktivitäten, letzteres aber nur bei sehr großen Unternehmen.

Wo dies gesetzlich angeordnet ist oder im Gesellschaftsvertrag so vorgesehen ist, wird der Prüfungsbericht der Unternehmensprüfer veröffentlicht, der die Korrektheit der Unternehmensangaben, namentlich der Bilanzen, bestätigt.

Obwohl das Gesetz nur wenig über die Pflichten der Unternehmensprüfer sagt, so haben die einzelnen Berufsorganisationen der verschiedenen als Prüfer zugelassenen Berufsgruppen Minimalstandards festgelegt, denen ein Prüfbericht zu entsprechen hat.

Regularien und ihre Überwachung

Der buchhalterische Gesamtprozess bestehend aus Einnahme-Überschuss-Rechnung, Bilanzierung, ggf. Prüfung und den verschiedenen begleitenden Berichten wird zusammenfassend als „Financial Reporting" bezeichnet. Da dieses einen großen Stellenwert im Hinblick auf die Bewertung von Unternehmen hat, muss es Regeln hierzu geben, deren Einhaltung überwacht wird. Hierbei geht es naturgemäß in erster Linie um gesetzliche Regeln, die in der Praxis freilich ergänzt werden durch Regeln, die sich die Berufsverbände der Wirtschaftsprüfer und Buchhalter gegeben haben sowie durch die Regularien der Börsenaufsicht. Folgende Institutionen schaffen den Rahmen für das „Financial Reporting" im Vereinigten Königreich bzw. überwachen dessen Einhaltung:
- Das **Parlament** ist verantwortlich für diejenige Gesetzgebung, die das financial reporting von Unter-

nehmen unmittelbar beeinflusst; dies betrifft in erster Linie den Companies Act 1985

- Die **Regierung** stößt die Gesetzgebungsverfahren an und übt über das Department of Trade and Industry (DIT) auch erheblichen Einfluss aus

- Das **Accounting Standards Board (ASB)** gibt Muster für Bilanzen und andere Dokumente heraus, die in den Prozess zur Schaffung der Financial Reporting Standards (FRSs) einmünden und als Standards of Accounting Practice (SSAPs) veröffentlicht werden

- 33Das **Financial Reporting Review Panel** untersucht die Bilanzen der Unternehmen, die fehlerhaft erscheinen

- Die **Börse** stellt Regeln für die Bilanzierung börsennotierter Gesellschaften auf

- Das **International Accounting Standards Committee (IASC)** gibt Empfehlungen für die Vereinheitlichung der Finanzberichterstattung von Unternehmen heraus

Grundsätzlich kann man nach dem Zweck der Regeln wie folgt unterscheiden:

- Regeln, die der vollständigen Hinterlegung aller erforderlichen Informationen dienen

- Regeln, die den erforderlichen Inhalt dieser Informationen präzisieren

- Regeln, die der Bewertung dienen.

Ursprünglich dienten die Regeln der Legislative (z.B. den Companies Act) in erster Linie dem Erfordernis der vollständigen Hinterlegung, während die des privaten Sektors sich mit dem Inhalt und der Bewertung befassten. Diese herkömmliche Aufteilung ist jedoch verwässert, seit der Companies Act 1981 das Erfordernis eines bestimmten Musters für die Einnahme-Überschuss-Rechnung vorschrieb. Es gibt mittlerweile zahlreiche weitere Beispiele für solche Durchbrechungen des althergebrachten Systems.

Gesetzliche Regeln

Die Geschichte der gesetzlichen Regelungen in England zur Rechnungslegung geht zurück bis auf den Joint Stock Companies Act von 1844. Den bis heute entscheidenden Einfluss auf das financial reporting haben freilich die Companies Acts von 1948, 1967 und 1981 ausgeübt. Die Vorschriften dieser Gesetze und ihrer Nachfolger aus den Jahren 1976 und 1980 wurden zum Companies Act 1985 verschmolzen, der heute in der Fassung von 1989 die tragenden gesetzlichen Rahmenbedingungen zum Financial Reporting enthält.[3]

Die Vorgänger-Gesetze von 1948 und 1967 haben die Grundsätze für die Rechnungslegung von Unternehmen und Unternehmern geschaffen, die in ihren wesentlichen Bestandteilen so heute noch gelten. Das Gesetz von 1948 hat darüber hinaus die Wirtschaftsprüfer verpflichtet, nicht nur die Bilanzen zu bestätigen sondern zu bescheinigen, dass das gesamte Financial Reporting eines Unternehmens korrekt ist. Im Rah-

---

[3] Die Vorschriften des CA 1985 für die Rechnungslegung und Buchführung sind in der Anlage abgedruckt, der Gesamttext ist unter der ISBN 3-937686-49-5 lieferbar.

men des Companies Act 1981 wurde der Grundsatz der Wahrheit und Offenheit der Bilanzen zum überragenden Grundprinzip der Gesetzgebung erhoben. Dies hat zur Folge, dass unter Umständen selbst Informationen, deren Preisgabe das Gesetz nicht ausdrücklich verlangt, offen gelegt werden müssen, wenn sie erforderlich sind, um einen umfassenden Überblick über die Situation des Unternehmens zu gewährleisten. Das Gesetz von 1981 enthält darüber hinaus die Verpflichtung, die spezifischen Vertriebskosten in der Einnahme-Überschuss-Rechnung anzugeben. Die wichtigste Neuerung des Companies Act 1981 war jedoch die Beschreibung der formellen Voraussetzungen, denen die Bereitstellung der finanziellen Informationen zu folgen hatte sowie die Definition der Grundprinzipien der Rechnungslegung von Unternehmen. Letztlich sind diese Ausprägungen Beispiele für den wachsenden Einfluss des Europäischen Rechts im Vereinigten Königreich.

Eines der erklärten Ziele der EU ist die Harmonisierung des Unternehmensrechts in den Mitgliedsstaaten. Dies wird in erster Linie durch die Umsetzung von Richtlinien der EU erreicht. Die wichtigste EU-Richtlinie war die sog. 4. Richtlinie zur Harmonisierung des Unternehmensrechts aus dem Jahre 1978, die eine Vielzahl von Regelungen über Inhalt, Form, Bewertungsansätzen und Veröffentlichung von Bilanzen aufstellte und die im wesentlichen mit dem Companies Act 1981 umgesetzt wurde. Dieser wurde in den Jahren 1985 und 1989 weiter novelliert.

Regelungen der Berufsverbände

Bis 1990 war es in erster Linie das ASC (Accounting Standards Committee), welches für die Aufstellung von Regeln zur Bilanzierung und Prüfung beitrug. Das ASC bestand aus den Vertretern der sechs größten Berufsverbände wirtschaftsprüfender und beratender Berufe im Vereinigten Königreich. 1990 wurde das ASC durch das ASB (Accounting Standards Board) ersetzt, das sich aus Vertretern der wirtschaftsprüfenden Berufe, der Finanzwirtschaft und der Regierung zusammensetzt. Die Ziele des ASB bestehen darin, Standards für das Financial Reporting zum Vorteil der Nutzer solcher Informationen aufzustellen und zu verbessern. Hierzu

- entwickelt das ASB Grundsätze und Rahmenbedingungen für das Financial Reporting
- gibt das ASB neue, verbesserte Regeln heraus, um hierdurch den veränderten Anforderungen einer dynamischen wirtschaft Rechnung zu tragen
- erstellt das ASB im Bedarfsfall Berichte zu dringenden Sachverhalten

Die Grundsätze des ASB wurden im ***Statement of Principles for Financial Reporting*** aus dem November 1995 festgelegt. Dort ist in 7 Kapiteln festgeschrieben, wie das Financial Reporting von Unternehmen aus dem Vereinigten Königreich zu erfolgen hat. Die Kapitel lauten wie folgt:

1. Ziele von Bilanzen
2. Qualitative Anforderungen an Bilanzen
3. Bestandteile von Bilanzen
4. Verpflichtungen in Bilanzen

5. Messwerte in Bilanzen
6. Präsentation von Bilanzen
7. Die berichtspflichtige Unternehmenseinheit

Die von der ASB herausgegebenen Regeln werden zusammenfassend **Financial Reporting Standards (FRSs)** genannt, die ebenfalls von ihr aufgelegten Muster **Financial Reporting Exposure Drafts (FREDs)**. Es existieren zwischenzeitlich eine Reihe von FRSs und FREDs sowie darüber hinaus eine Reihe von Diskussionspapieren, die den jeweiligen Erörterungsstand aktueller Vorhaben widerspiegeln.

Eilmeldungen gibt das ASB durch die UITF **(Urgend Issues Task Force**, s. o.) heraus. Die Hauptaufgabe der UITF besteht darin, Situationen zu erkennen, in denen kurzfristiger Handlungsbedarf besteht. Dies kann etwa der Fall sein, wenn streitige Interpretationen von existierenden Vorschriften auftreten oder die Rechtswirklichkeit eine rasche Anpassung der Normen erforderlich macht. In dem Fall wird der Konsens aller Beteiligten gesucht und anschließend als **Consensus Pronouncement** veröffentlicht, das dann verbindlichen Charakter hat.

Regeln der Wertpapierbörse

Der Rat der Wertpapierbörse fordert, dass die veröffentlichten Bilanzen der an der Börse gelisteten Unternehmen über den gesetzlichen Rahmen hinausgehende Informationen enthalten. Die betrifft z.B. die sonst nicht erforderliche Erklärung, ob die Bilanzen im Einklang mit dem **Cadbury Committees Code** (siehe oben) erstellt wurden. Es wird darüber hinaus erwartet, dass Unternehmen freiwillig und begründet erklären, warum sie ggf. von den anerkannten Regeln der Bilanzierung abweichen, auch wenn dies gesetzlich im Einzelfall zulässig sein sollte.

Regeln des IASC

Das ***International Accounting Standards Committee*** (IASC) wurde 1973 von neun Staaten eingerichtet; 1997 war es auf 199 Mitglieder aus 88 Ländern angewachsen. Ziel des IASC ist die Harmonisierung des Financial Reporting. Hierzu formuliert und veröffentlicht das IASC (unverbindliche) Regelungen (***International Accounting Standards, IASs***) und wirbt für ihre Einhaltung bzw. Implementierung in die nationale Gesetzgebung.

Insgesamt ist der Einfluss des IASC im Vereinigten Königreich vergleichsweise gering. Dies liegt in erster Linie an der Freiwilligkeit der Umsetzung der Regeln. Hinzu kommt, dass die IASs in der Regel mehrere Wege erlauben, das Financial Reporting zu erledigen, was einer allgemeinverbindlichen Regelung ebenfalls im Wege steht.

Dies mag sich zukünftig infolge der Vereinbarung mit der ***International Organisation of Securities Commission (IOSCO)*** aus dem Jahre 1995 ändern, wonach die IASC einen Kernbereich von Regeln erarbeitet, die für große multinationale Unternehmen bindend sein sollen.

Andere Einflüsse

In den letzten Jahren hat sich der Focus dahin entwickelt, aus den veröffentlichten Bilanzen der Unternehmen Rückschlüsse auf deren soziales Verhalten zu ziehen (wie z.B. die Beschäftigung von Minderheiten). Gleiches gilt für das Umweltverhalten von Unternehmen. So erteilen etliche Unternehmen hierüber freiwillige Auskünfte, indem sie die Pflichtangaben entsprechend ergänzen.

In den letzten Jahren sind die gesetzlichen Bestimmungen hierzu verschärft worden. Dies betrifft Aspekte zur Gesundheit und Sicherheit am Arbeitsplatz sowie die Beschäftigungspolitik.

Dies alles hat zu der Anregung geführt, dass Unternehmen grundsätzlich weg vom reinen Financial Accounting hin zu einer weiten, umfassenden Bilanzierung ihrer Aktivitäten übergehen sollten. Diese Form der Information wird gemeinhin als „Social Reporting" bezeichnet, sie hat jedoch aus den verschiedensten Gründen (Komplexität, Kosten, unterschiedliche Interessenlage je nach Größe und Branche) keine Verbreitung gefunden.

Ein weiteres Phänomen der letzten Jahre ist die Zunahme sog. „off-balance-sheet-finance" bzw. "window-dressing-schemes".

Ersteres ist dann der Fall, wenn der Geschäftsbetrieb eines Unternehmens in einer Weise finanziert wird, der auch unter Zugrundelegung der gesetzlichen Vorschriften über die Bilanzierung zur Folge hat, dass diese Finanzaktivitäten sich in der Bilanz des Unternehmens nicht wieder finden.

Von „window-dressing-schemes" spricht man, wenn gezielt Transaktionen vorgenommen werden, die nicht oder nur teilweise in den Bilanzen auftauchen und daher ein irreführendes oder gar verfälschendes Bild der finanziellen Situation herbeiführen.

Beide Phänomene haben, nachdem sie verstärkt in der Praxis auftraten, das ASC auf den Plan gerufen und zwei Bekanntmachungen (ED 42 aus 1988 und ED 49 aus 1990, später FRED 4 bzw. FRS 5) zur Folge, wonach in jedem Fall alle Finanztransaktionen gleich welcher Art und Form nach ihrer Substanz und nicht nach formellen Gesichtspunkten zu richten haben („Reporting the substance of transactions"). Wesentlich ist daher, dass eine englische Bilanz die ökonomische Realität widerspiegelt.

Das gesamte oben dargestellte Regelwerk wird oftmals auch als **UK GAAP (Generally Accepted Accounting Practices)** bezeichnet, wobei zu beachten ist, dass der Begriff GAAP im Vereinigten Königreich eine wesentlich undeutlichere Definition enthält als etwa in den USA und Kanada.

BILANZIERUNGSRICHTLINIEN

Wie dargestellt, ist das Regelwerk zur Rechnungslegung von Unternehmen im Vereinigten Königreich einerseits umfangreich, andererseits aber auch lückenhaft und auslegungsbedürftig. Es arbeitet mit dem gelegentlich unklaren Begriff der substantiellen Richtigkeit von Unternehmensbilanzen, einem Begriff, der im Einzelfall durchaus verschiedene Wertungen zulässt. In der Unternehmenspraxis haben sich daher verschiedene Rechnungslegungsprinzipien etabliert, die je nach Lage des Falles ggf. auch kumulativ Anwendung finden. Die wichtigsten Prämissen sind die folgenden:

- getrennte Bilanzen für jedes Unternehmen
- Bewertung immer nur in Geld
- Dauerhaftigkeit der Unternehmenstätigkeit
- Anschaffungskosten statt Zeitwert
- Gewinnbilanzierung erst bei Realisierung
- Verlustbilanzierung bereits bei Verlustentstehung
- Verteilung von Aufwendungen auf Bilanzperiode
- Einheitlichkeit der Bilanz
- Prinzip der konservativen Bilanzierung
- Nur wesentliche Informationen gehören in die Bilanz

Im Einzelnen:

Das Prinzip getrennter Unternehmenseinheiten

Nach dem englischen Gesellschaftsrecht werden juristische Personen (wie die Limited) grundsätzlich isoliert von ihren Gesellschaftern behandelt. Es ist daher ein akzeptiertes Prinzip, immer für jede Einheit gesondert zu bilanzieren. Zu Konzernbilanzen kommen wir später.

Bewertung in Geld

Das sog. money measurement Prinzip besteht darin, lediglich solche Vorgänge in eine Bilanz aufzunehmen, die einen in Geld messbaren Einfluss auf die Finanzen eines Unternehmens haben können. Dies schließt z.B. aus, die Qualität der Unternehmenstätigkeit in der Bilanz erscheinen zu lassen. Erst wenn sich diese Qualität in erhöhten Erlösen widerspiegelt, findet sie - indirekt- Eingang in das Rechnungswesen. Auch werden naturgemäß die Kosten für Aus- und Weiterbildung oder Zertifizierungsmaßnahmen bilanziert, da sie einen unmittelbaren Geldwert haben.

Geld ist ein offensichtlicher und einleuchtender Messwert, der anders als rein ideelle Werte in aller Regel Vergleichbarkeit bietet. Auf der anderen Seite behält Geld erfahrungsgemäß nicht seinen Wert, insbesondere nicht in Zeiten der Inflation. Hinzu kommt, dass z.B. der bei florierenden Geschäften oftmals bedeutende Unternehmenswert (der „goodwill") nicht ohne weiteres in Geld erfasst werden kann. Hier handelt es sich um eine unbestimmte, durch eine Vielzahl von Faktoren abhängige Größe, die regelmäßig nicht objektiv dargestellt werden kann und die darüber hinaus stärker als andere Faktoren der Konjunktur und anderen Faktoren unterliegt. Letzteres wird ausnahmsweise dann bilanziert, wenn es virulent wird - also etwa im Falle eines Unternehmenskaufs.

Dennoch wird diese Abgrenzung in der Praxis flexibel gehandhabt. So ist es z.B. zulässig, Markennamen von Unternehmen, die einen merkantilen Wert haben, zu bewerten und regelmäßig zu bilanzieren, obwohl es sich hier um ideelle, nicht ohne weiteres und insbesondere nicht ohne Zwischenschaltung eines Bewertungsvorgangs in Geld zu übersetzende Werte handelt. Auf der anderen Seite können etablierte Markennamen einen erheblichen Wert ausmachen, dessen Nichtberücksichtigung die Bilanz verfälschen würde.

Dauerhaftigkeit des Unternehmens

Das Bilanzrecht unterstellt regelmäßig die dauerhafte Fortführung des Unternehmens über den jeweiligen Bilanzierungszeitraum hinaus. Andernfalls wäre etwa die jahrelange Abschreibung von hochwertigen Gütern nicht möglich, die naturgemäß die Fortdauer des Unternehmens für den restlichen Abschreibungszeitraum antizipiert.

Anschaffungskosten statt Zeitwert

Ursprünglich ging man beim Wertansatz von Wirtschaftsgütern in Unternehmensbilanzen von deren Anschaffungskosten aus. Das hatte den Vorteil eines klar definierten, für jedermann nachvollziehbaren Wertansatzes, führte aber dann zu Problemen, wenn sich der tatsächliche Wert des Wirtschaftsgutes tatsächlich von dem Anschaffungspreis entfernte. Dies würde dem dargestellten Grundsatz der Wahrheit und Klarheit von Bilanzen widersprechen. Es hat daher verschiedene Ansätze gegeben, neben den Anschaffungskosten auch den Zeitwert zu berücksichtigen, durchgesetzt haben sich diese freilich in der Praxis nicht. Es ist den Unternehmen aber gestattet, Wirtschaftsgüter periodisch zu bewerten und diesen Wertansatz in der Bilanz anzusetzen.

Gewinnbilanzierung bei Realisierung

Ein weiterer Grundsatz des Bilanzrechts besteht darin, Wertzuwächse erst dann zu bilanzieren, wenn sie realisiert wurden. Gewinnerwartungen genügen nicht. Realisierung bedeutet freilich nicht, dass Geld fließen muss, es genügt, dass ein bindender Kaufvertrag über den Vermögensgegenstand geschlossen wird.

Verlustbilanzierung bei Entstehung

Es gilt ganz allgemein, dass Einnahmen und Ausgaben dann verbucht werden, wenn sie entstehen, nicht jedoch erst, wenn sie bezahlt oder anders erfüllt werden. Es kommt also maßgeblich auf den Zeitpunkt des Entstehens einer Forderung oder Verpflichtung an, nicht aber auf deren spätere Erfüllung.

Verteilung von Aufwendungen auf Bilanzperioden

Grundsätzlich müssen Einnahmen und Ausgaben gemeinsam bilanziert werden. Auf der anderen Seite entstehen die Kosten meist zu einem früheren Zeitpunkt, lange bevor die Gewinne realisiert werden können. Dies führt beinahe zwangsläufig zu einer Verfälschung der Bilanz, die zu einem bestimmten fixen Zeitpunkt aufgestellt wird. Die Schwierigkeit besteht also darin, festzustellen, welche Bilanzierungszeiträume von welchen Aufwendungen profitieren. Wenn zum Beispiel eine langlebige Maschine angeschafft wird, deren Kaufpreis sofort bezahlt wird, die aber dem Unternehmen über Jahre hilft, Erlöse zu erzielen, so muss der Anschaffungspreis bilanztechnisch auf verschiedene Zeiträume verteilt werden, was in der Praxis aber nicht immer exakt möglich ist.

Grundsätzlich werden Bilanzen für einen bestimmten, festgelegten und immer wiederkehrenden Zeitraum erstellt. Dieser Zeitraum beträgt in der Regel ein Jahr und deckt sich mit dem Kalenderjahr. Dies führt naturgemäß zu den bereits oben angesprochenen Problemen, wenn z. B. einzelne Geschäftstätigkeiten nicht innerhalb eines Jahres abgeschlossen sind, wie dies etwa in der Bauindustrie bei größeren Vorhaben regelmäßig der Fall ist. In dem Fall muss das Vorhaben entsprechend dem Stand zum Ende der jeweiligen Periode bewertet werden.

Einheitlichkeit der Bilanz

Im Recht der Bilanzbuchhaltung gibt es oftmals verschiedene Möglichkeiten, Vermögensgegenstände oder Vermögenswerte zu bewerten. Das gleiche gilt z. B. für die Aufteilung von Aufwendungen auf verschiedene Bilanzperioden. Beispiele hierfür werden in Kapitel 2 erläutert. Das Prinzip der Einheitlichkeit verlangt, dass sowohl innerhalb der einzelnen Bilanzperioden als auch von einer Periode zur nächsten die Bewertungsansätze grundsätzlich in der gleichen Weise vorgenommen werden, dass willkürliche Unterschiede vermieden werden. Sobald sich ein Unternehmer also für eine zulässige Bewertungsmethode entschieden hat, muss er diese beibehalten und darf sich nicht willkürlich für eine andere entscheiden, da dies die Vergleichbarkeit der fortlaufenden Bilanzen beeinträchtigen würde.

Prinzip der konservativen Bilanzierung

Die Erstellung von Bilanzen erfordert oftmals Bewertungen, die naturgemäß einen Ermessensspielraum eröffnen. Dieser soll konservativ genutzt werden, das heißt, dass grundsätzlich ein zurückhaltender und vorsichtiger Ansatz in Bezug auf Bewertungen, insbesondere in Bezug auf Gewinnerwartungen, erforderlich ist. Hinzu kommt, dass sämtliche Verbindlichkeiten, sobald sie bekannt werden, unverzüglich in die Bilanz aufgenommen werden. Im Gegenzug dürfen Gewinne erst dann bilanziert werden, wenn sie realisiert werden, Gewinnerwartungen alleine sind daher nicht bilanzierungsfähig (s.o.).

Nur wesentliche Informationen

Grundsätzlich finden nur solche Informationen, die einen Einfluss auf Entscheidungen der Benutzer von Bilanzen haben können, Eingang in Bilanzen. Informationen, die hierüber hinausgehen, sollen nicht in Bilanzen erscheinen. So können zu viele Detailinformationen unter Umständen ein klares Bild von der ökonomischen Lage eines Unternehmens verwässern, was natürlich auch dann gilt, wenn zu wenige oder unzureichende Informationen präsentiert werden. Wann welche Informationen erforderlich, aber auch ausreichend sind, kann nur anhand der Umstände des Einzelfalles entschieden werden. Es liegt auf der Hand, dass dies auch entscheidend von der Unternehmensgröße und der Unternehmensstruktur abhängt. So kann bei einem kleinen Unternehmen eine Transaktion im Wert von 100 Pfund bedeutsam sein, bei einem großen Unternehmen eine im Wert von 1 Mio. Pfund hingegen relativ unbedeutend. Wer mit der Erstellung der Bilanzen befasst ist, muss eine professionelle Entscheidung über die Relevanz jeder einzelnen Information treffen. Hierbei kommt es entscheidend darauf an, ob die Verwender einer Bilanz diese Information benötigen, um einen zutreffenden Eindruck von der Finanzlage des betroffenen Unternehmens zu gewinnen.

***

Zusammenfassend kann man sagen, dass das englische Bilanzrecht vergleichsweise offen ist. Es existiert eine Reihe von allgemein akzeptierten Bilanzierungsgrundsätzen, die angewendet werden können, ohne dass die Bilanz fehlerhaft wäre. Maßgeblich ist immer das Prinzip der materiellen Korrektheit der Bilanz, das über Formfragen steht. Gleichwohl wird häufig kritisiert, dass im Vereinigten Königreich der Grundsatz der Verlässlichkeit und Zuverlässigkeit der Informationen einen höheren Stellenwert hat als derjenige der möglichst hohen Nutzbarkeit von Informationen in Bilanzen. Im Übrigen muss man immer im Auge behalten, dass das englische Bilanzrecht wegen seiner nur geringen gesetzlichen Vorgaben in besonderem Maße der Evolution und damit auch der Veränderung unterliegt.

FORMVORSCHRIFTEN

Bilanzen unterliegen darüber hinaus naturgemäß Formvorschriften, die einzuhalten sind. Dabei ist zu unterscheiden zwischen solchen, die zwingend den Inhalt und die Struktur von Bilanzen regeln und solchen, die sich mit - fakultativen - Jahresberichten befassen.

Zwingende Form

Der Companies Act 1985 schreibt vor, dass Bilanzen und Einnahme-Überschuss-Rechnungen den dort normierten Vorgaben zu entsprechen haben. Für Bilanzen gibt es zwei alternative Muster, für Einnahme-Überschuss-Rechnungen vier. Alle werden später im Einzelnen auch anhand von Mustern erläutert (siehe Anlagen)

Wer einmal eine bestimmte Vorlage gewählt hat, muss diese fortführen, es sei denn, es gibt im Einzelfall gewichtige Gründe für ein Abweichen. Auf jeden Fall müssen Vergleichswerte in verschiedenen Bilanzen zwingend im jeweils gleichen Muster präsentiert werden.

Für jede Vorlage sind die einzelnen Vorgaben bis hin zur Reihenfolge, in der die Angaben zu erfolgen haben, zwingend einzuhalten. Diese stellen Mindeststandards dar, die freilich freiwillig überschritten werden können. So können Angaben detaillierter als erforderlich erfolgen oder können zusätzliche Angaben gemacht werden, sofern der Tätigkeitsbereich des Unternehmens dies erforderlich erscheinen lässt, um einen korrekten und umfassenden Überblick über sein Rechnungswesen zu erhalten.

Jahresberichte

Von Bilanzen abzugrenzen sind die in der Regel freiwilligen Unternehmensberichte, in denen freiwillige Angaben - meist für potentielle Investoren - in Hochglanzform gemacht werden. Oftmals enthalten diese sog. Jahresberichte auch die Bilanz, aber eben auch eine ganze Reihe darüber hinausgehender Informationen. Große Unternehmen machen hiervon in aller Regel Gebrauch, kleinere nicht. Wer nicht an der Börse notiert ist, braucht in der Regel keinen Jahresbericht.

DIE EINNAHME-ÜBERSCHUSSRECHNUNG

Die Einnahme-Überschuss-Rechnung wird oftmals auch als „income statement" bezeichnet. Sie fasst die Ergebnisse der Geschäftstätigkeiten des Unternehmens in der relevanten Periode (meist ein Kalenderjahr) zusammen. Sie erfasst Verkäufe oder Umsätze, laufende Betriebsaufwendungen, besondere Betriebsaufwendungen, Zinsaufwendungen, steuerliche Aufwendungen und Dividenden. Die Einnahme-Überschuss-Rechnung hat den großen Anreiz, dass ihr rechnerisches Ergebnis bereits einen ersten recht guten Eindruck über das wirtschaftliche Ergebnis des Unternehmens vermittelt, der auch dem Laien gut vermittelbar ist.

Dieses Kapitel erläutert die verschiedenen Möglichkeiten, eine Einnahme-Überschuss-Rechnung abzufassen, welche im Companies Act 1985 in der heute geltenden Fassung vorgesehen sind und erklärt, welche Elemente enthalten sein müssen. Darüber hinaus werden insbesondere die Erfordernisse, die sich aus der sog. FRS 3 („Reporting Finance Performance") auf die Erstellung der Einnahme-Überschuss-Rechnung ergeben, dargestellt.

Zulässige Muster

Die zulässigen Muster von Einnahme-Überschuss-Rechnungen sind abschließend im Anhang zum Companies Act 1985 erläutert. Erstmals wurden diese Muster 1981 festgelegt, obgleich die Verwendung standardisierter Vorlagen für Einnahme-Überschuss-Rechnungen in der EU seit Jahren anerkannte Praxis ist. Im Vereinigten Königreich bedeutete diese Umstellung eine Neuorientierung, die seinerzeit nicht unumstritten war. Der Vorteil von Vorlagen liegt auf der Hand: Gute Vergleichbarkeit und die Sicherstellung von Mindestinhalten. Auf der anderen Seite führt die Vereinheitlichung zum Verlust an Möglichkeiten, einzelne Konten in der Weise zu präsentieren, wie das unter Umständen aus der besonderen Situation einzelner Unternehmen heraus geboten wäre.

Derzeit stehen vier verschiedene Muster für die Einnahme-Überschuss-Rechnung zur Verfügung. [4]

Bei den Mustern 1 und 3 handelt es sich um einfache Vorlagen, die sich von den Mustern 2 und 4 dadurch unterscheiden, dass letztere die notwenigen Informationen nach Ein- und Ausgaben klassifiziert, während erstere die Einordnung von Buchungsposten nach der Funktion vornehmen. Grundsätzlich lässt sich folgende Unterscheidung treffen: Die Muster 1 und 3 erfordern die Aufteilung der operativen Ausgaben in

- Herstellungskosten
- Vertriebskosten
- Verwaltungskosten,

während die Muster 2 und 4 eine weitere Diversifizierung der operativen Aufwendungen vorsehen in:

- Veränderungen im Bestand fertiger und halbfertiger Waren
- own work capitalized

---

[4] alle im Anhang abgedruckt

- Roh- und Verbrauchsmaterial
- andere Fremdkosten
- Personalkosten
- Abschreibungen auf Sachanlagen und immaterielle Werte
- Sonderabschreibungen
- andere Betriebskosten

Hieraus ist ersichtlich, dass die Verwendung der Muster 2 und 4 die Kalkulation von Herstellungskosten deutlich verkompliziert. Bei vielen Unternehmen ist der Rohertrag ein wesentlicher Bewertungsmaßstab, dessen Errechnung unter Maßgabe der Muster 2 und 4 nur möglich ist, wenn Informationen über Abschreibungen, Arbeitskosten und sonstiger Betriebskosten zugänglich sind. In vielen Fällen sind daher die - ohnehin einfacheren - Muster 1 und 3 zu bevorzugen.

Grundsätzlich sollen natürlich die Muster gewählt werden, die für das betreffende Unternehmen am besten passen. Hierbei ist zu berücksichtigen, dass der Erläuterungsbedarf bei den Mustern 2 und 4 aus den genannten Gründen erheblich größer ist als bei den anderen Mustern. Im Vereinigten Königreich wählen die meisten Unternehmen das Muster 1 als Vorlage für ihre Einnahme-Überschuss-Rechnung.

Die Gliederung innerhalb der Muster erfolgt entweder nach Buchstaben (A, B, C, etc.), römischen (I, II, III, etc.) oder arabischen Zahlen (1, 2, 3, etc.). Diese Nummerierung ist in allen Mustern vorgegeben und muss zwingend übernommen werden. Weitere - im Muster nicht vorgesehene - Punkte können zusätzlich aufgenommen werden. Eine gewisse Flexibilität ist hinsichtlich der Frage gegeben, welche Informationen in der Aufstellung und welche in den Anmerkungen („Notes") erfolgen dürfen. Sachliche Unterschiede sind hiermit allerdings nicht verbunden, Maßstab ist allein die Übersichtlichkeit und Vergleichbarkeit mit früheren und anderen Einnahme-Überschuss-Rechnungen. Grundlegende Informationen müssen ohnehin immer in der Aufstellung selber enthalten sein und dürfen nicht im Anhang „versteckt" werden.

Einzelpositionen in den Mustern

Im Folgenden werden die einzelnen Positionen in den verschiedenen Mustern erläutert. Im Regelfall betreffen die Erläuterungen alle Muster in gleicher Weise; wo dies nicht der Fall ist, wird darauf hingewiesen.

Umsatz („Turnover")

Es liegt auf der Hand, dass die Angabe des Unternehmensumsatzes essentieller Bestandteil jeder Einnahme-Überschuss-Rechnung und jeder Bilanz ist. Bei konsolidierten Bilanzen entfallen diejenigen Umsätze, die innerhalb der Gruppe verbundener Unternehmen erzielt werden, es werden also nur Außenumsätze erfasst.

Grundsätzlich ist weiter erforderlich, zwischen Umsätzen aus normalem Geschäftsbetrieb (continuing operations), Akquisitionen (als Teil des normalen Geschäftsbetriebs) und beendeten Geschäftsvorgängen (discontinued operations) zu unterscheiden. Beendete Geschäftsvorgänge werden definiert als solche, die entweder innerhalb der Berichtsperiode verkauft oder eingestellt wurden; gleiches gilt für Geschäftsvorgänge, die innerhalb von drei Monaten nach Beginn der folgenden Periode oder aber innerhalb von drei Monaten vor Prüfung der Bilanz beendet wurden, je nachdem, welches Ereignis früher eintritt. Die Beendigung muss ihrerseits dauerhaft sein und darf nicht nur eine Unterbrechung auf Zeit darstellen. Außerdem müssen die beendeten Geschäftsvorgänge einschließlich aller dazu gehörenden Vermögenswerte klar und eindeutig vom laufenden Geschäft abgrenzbar und damit identifizierbar sein.

Akquisitionen werden definiert als Unternehmungen oder Unternehmen, die das bilanzierende Unternehmen in der Berichtsperiode erworben hat. Erfasst wird daher hier nur externes, nicht jedoch internes Wachstum.

Weiterhin müssen die Umsatzangaben in der Einnahme-Überschuss-Rechnung dann aufgeteilt werden, wenn sie aus unterschiedlichen Geschäftsbereichen oder verschiedenen Regionen stammen, in denen das Unternehmen operiert. In der Regel ist das erforderlich, wenn 10% oder mehr des Umsatzes eines Unternehmens aus einem solcherart abgrenzbaren Bereich stammen. In diesem Fall ist weiterhin zwischen Umsätzen nach regionaler Herkunft und Umsätzen nach regionalem Absatz zu unterscheiden.

Der Grund für diese relativ weitgehende Forderung nach regionaler Segmentierung des Umsatzes in der Einnahme-Überschuss-Rechnung liegt darin, dass diese Informationen insbesondere bei größeren Unternehmen für die Beurteilung der wirtschaftlichen Lage von entscheidender Bedeutung sein können. Insbesondere spezielle Risiken lassen sich so schneller identifizieren.

Herstellungskosten (Cost of Sales)

Die Muster 1 und 3 für die Einnahme-Überschuss-Rechnung verlangen die separate Aufführung von Herstellungskosten. Hierzu zählen im Regelfall alle Kosten, die mit dem gewöhnlichen Geschäftsbetrieb des Unternehmens verbunden sind. Dies sind etwa:

- Aufwendungen für Lagerbestände und unfertige Arbeiten
- Aufwendungen für Material oder Beschaffung
- andere externe Kosten
- Arbeitskosten
- der Herstellung zuzuordnende Verwaltungskosten
- Abschreibung und Wertminderung von Produktionsanlagen und anderen der Produktion zuzurodnenden Vermögenswerte
- Aufwand für Forschung und Entwicklung

Unfertige Arbeiten müssen hierbei naturgemäß bewertet werden.

Für Handelsunternehmen werden die Beschaffungskosten (Einkauf) das wesentliche Element sein, bei produzierenden Unternehmen bekommen Aufwendungen wie Arbeitskraft, Abschreibungen und Energiekosten regelmäßig einen höheren Stellenwert.

Material und Beschaffung

Sobald Material eingekauft wird, sei es für den Wiederverkauf oder für die Weiterverarbeitung, wird es dem Vermögenswert „Lager" zugeordnet. Diese Lagerware wird unter Umständen weiterverkauft und durch neue ersetzt. Dies alles kann innerhalb einer Berichtsperiode sehr häufig erfolgen, erschwert aber naturgemäß die am Ende der Berichtsperiode erforderliche Feststellung der Kosten für Material und Beschaffung. Üblicherweise wird es wie folgt kalkuliert:

Lagerbestand am Beginn der Berichtsperiode zuzüglich der Einkäufe in der Berichtsperiode abzüglich des Lagerbestandes am Ende des Berichtszeitraumes.

Aufgrund der Vielzahl einzelner Verfügungen über den Lagerbestand im Laufe eines Jahres ist es häufig unmöglich, festzustellen, welche Ware sich am Lager befindet und welche bereits verkauft oder verarbeitet wurde. Aus bilanztechnischen Gründen ist diese Feststellung jedenfalls bei identischer Ware aber auch gar nicht erforderlich, hier genügt die Feststellung anhand der genannten Formel zum Bilanzstichtag. Dies gilt freilich dann nicht mehr, wenn sich im Laufe des Berichtszeitraumes die Preise verändert haben. Dann hilft man sich mit der Annahme „first in - first out", wonach im Regelfall diejenige Lagerware, die zuerst angeschafft wird, auch zuerst verkauft wird. Je nach Branchenusus kann aber auch die Annahme „last in - first out" Anwendung finden, wonach immer zuerst die aktuellste Ware abverkauft wird. Schließlich gibt es - bei homogenen Massengütern, etwa Schrauben - die Möglichkeit, den wert über das durchschnittliche Gewicht zu bestimmen. Letzteres ist aber nur dann zulässig, wenn der Einfluss auf die Einnahme-Überschuss-Rechnung gering und andere Evaluierungsmöglichkeiten nur mit unzumutbarem Aufwand verbunden wären. Bei hohen Lagerbeständen und sich deutlich ändernden Preisen kann es durchaus einen erheblichen Einfluss auf die Einnahme-Überschuss-Rechnung haben, welche Annahme man wählt, im Regelfall des kleinen Unternehmens stellt sich dieses Problem allerdings nicht.

Abschreibungen

Fixe Vermögenswerte (wie etwa Betriebsgebäude, Produktionsanlagen, Fahrzeuge etc.) haben in der Regel eine Lebens- und Nutzungsdauer, die deutlich über eine Bilanzperiode hinausgeht. Außerdem ist in den meisten Fällen absehbar, dass solche Anlagen verschleißen, einer Wertminderung unterliegen und eines Tages aufgrund der fortgesetzten Nutzung überhaupt nicht mehr verwendbar sind. Es ist daher erforderlich, die Aufwendungen für diese Vermögenswerte in möglichst realistischer Weise auf die jeweiligen Bilanzzeiträume zu verteilen. Dieser Vorgang wird mit dem Begriff der Abschreibung erfasst. Hierbei ist eine Vorab-Einschätzung des Wertverlustes und der Nutzungsdauer des jeweiligen Vermögenswertes erforderlich, der je nach Wahl des verwendeten Musters für die Einnahme-Überschuss-Rechnung entweder in der Rechnung selber (Muster 2 und 4) oder in den Erläuterungen (Muster 1 und 3) zu erfolgen hat. Grundsätzlich geht die Berechnung der Abschreibung vom Anschaffungswert des Vermögensgegenstandes aus und setzt dem den voraussichtlichen Restwert nach Anlauf der voraussichtlichen Nutzungsdauer entgegen. Die Berechnung der Abschreibung setzt daher die Kenntnis oder Einschätzung folgender Faktoren voraus:

- Anschaffungspreis oder Werteinschätzung bei Anschaffung
- Restwert
- Nutzungsdauer

Dies verdeutlicht, dass die Berechnung der Abschreibung in erheblichem Maße einen Beurteilungsspielraum eröffnet, bevor überhaupt eine der gleich erläuterten Methoden zur Verteilung der Abschreibung auf die einzelnen Bilanzperioden Anwendung findet. Die betrifft in erster Linie die voraussichtliche Nutzungsdauer und - noch mehr - den Restwert des Vermögensgegenstandes.

Für die Verteilung der Abschreibung auf Bilanzperioden existieren verschiedene Berechnungsmöglichkeiten. Am weitesten verbreitet sind zwei Methoden: Die lineare Berechnungsmethode, die unterstellt, dass die Wertminderung über den gesamten Abschreibungszeitraum in gleicher Weise verteilt wird und die degressive Methode, die unterstellt, dass die Wertminderung in den ersten Jahren höher ist als in den späteren. Speziell bei Fahrzeugen entspricht dies in den meisten Fällen der kaufmännischen Realität.

Die Unterschiede, die sich aus den verschiedenen Berechnungsmethoden ergeben, können erheblich sein.

Beispiel:

Ein Fahrzeug wird zum Anschaffungspreis von 30.000 £ angeschafft, die Nutzungsdauer beträgt 5 Jahre, der Restwert nach 5 Jahren 5.000 £.

Jährliche Abschreibung: £ 30.000 - £ 5.000 ./. 5 = £ 5.000.

Würde man das Fahrzeug degressiv abschreiben, sähe das Bild anders aus. Zwar blieben Anschaffungspreis, Verkaufspreis und Nutzungsdauer gleich, allerdings muss hier der prozentuale Abschreibungssatz ermittelt werden. Dies geschieht mittels folgender Formel, wobei **n** die Nutzungsdauer in Jahren ist.

$$1 - \sqrt[n]{\left(\frac{Verkaufswert}{Anschaffungskosten}\right)}$$

In unserem Beispiel ergibt dies eine jährliche Abschreibung von ca. 30%.

$$1 - \sqrt[5]{\left(\frac{5.000}{30.000}\right)} \approx 30\%$$

In absoluten Zahlen würde dies folgendes bedeuten:

Jahr	Buchwert zu Jahresbeginn		Satz		jährliche Abschreibung	Buchwert zum Jahresende
2005	30.000	x	30%	=	9.000	21.000
2006	21.000	x	30%	=	6.300	14.700
2007	14.700	x	30%	=	4.410	10.290
2008	10.290	x	30%	=	3.087	7.203

2009	7.203	x	30%	=	2.161	5.042

Insbesondere in den ersten und letzten beiden Jahren ist der Unterschied zur linearen Abschreibung deutlich. Im ersten Jahr ist die jährliche Abschreibung fast doppelt so hoch.

Neben diesen beiden - anerkannten - Methoden der Abschreibung von Wirtschaftsgütern existieren weitere Berechnungsmodelle, die naturgemäß weiteren Spielraum für die Nutzung von Vorteilen gewähren. Hierbei darf bei aller Flexibilität und Liberalität des englischen Rechtssystems nicht übersehen werden, dass auch hier der Grundsatz gilt, wonach Bilanzen unbedingt der Wahrheit zu entsprechen haben und allen Nutzern ein objektives Bild von der finanziellen Lage des Unternehmens vermitteln müssen. Diese Maxime prägt auch hier die Entscheidung, welche Methode man letztlich zu wählen hat.

Verwaltungskosten (Distribution Costs)

Verwaltungskosten müssen unter allen zugelassenen Mustern für Einnahme-Überschuss-Rechnungen separat aufgeführt und analysiert werden. Typischerweise enthalten sie

- Gehälter und Gehaltsnebenkosten, Aufwendungen für soziale Sicherheit, Bonuszahlungen etc.
- Aufwendungen für Verwaltungsgebäude einschließlich Abschreibung
- Aufwendungen für Rechts- und Steuerberatung und ähnliche Aufwendungen

- Als unrealisierbar abgeschriebene Forderungen

Sonstiges operatives Einkommen (other operating income)

Auch die Rubrik des sonstigen operativen Einkommens erscheint in allen vier Mustern für die Einnahme-Überschuss-Rechnung, wenngleich sie in der Praxis keine große Bedeutung hat. Es handelt sich hier gleichsam um das Auffangbecken bisher nicht erfasster Umsätze. Beispiele hierfür sind

- Einnahmen aus Vermietung und Verpachtung von überschüssigem Gewerberaum
- Einnahmen aus Verkäufen in einer Betriebskantine

Einnahmen aus Beteiligungen an verbundenen Unternehmen

Hält das bilanzierende Unternehmen einen Anteil an einem anderen Unternehmen, mit dem es verbunden ist, so stellen sich eine Reihe besonderer Fragen in Bezug auf die Einnahme-Überschuss-Rechnung.

Unternehmen sind dann verbunden, wenn ein Unternehmen über das andere Kontrolle ausüben kann. Diese Kontrollmöglichkeit kann auf Mehrheitsbeteiligung beruhen (sog. „legal ownership"), sie kann aber auch auf faktischer Kontrolle der unternehmerischen Tätigkeit oder der Finanzpolitik eines Unternehmens begründet sein, sofern diese Kontrolle auf Dauer angelegt und strukturell in irgendeiner Form abgesichert ist. Diese Kontrolle kann natürlich auch durch mehrere Unternehmen gemeinsam ausgeübt werden. Unter Umständen - etwa bei Unternehmen in Streubesitz - kann sich auch schon deutlich unter halb einer Beteiligung von 50% angenommen werden, wenn die Minderheitsbeteiligung faktisch zur Kontrollmöglichkeit führt.

Sobald eine solche Verbundenheit von Unternehmen (=Konzern) festgestellt wird, müssen Konzernbilanzen („group accounts") erstellt werden. Der Konzern bilanziert, als würde es sich um ein einheitliches Einzelunternehmen handeln. Dies geschieht, indem die Einzelbilanzen der verbundenen Unternehmen konsolidiert, also zusammengeführt werden. Geschieht dies, was der Regelfall ist, bedarf es nicht mehr des gesonderten Ausweises von konzerninternen Umsätzen; diese sind irrelevant und brauchen in der Konzernbilanz auch nicht aufzuscheinen. Lediglich in dem sehr seltenen Fall der Nicht-Konsolidierung im Konzern bedarf es hier des gesonderten Ausweises.

Einnahmen aus sonstigen Beteiligungen

Unter einem Beteiligungsunternehmen wird ein solches Unternehmen verstanden, an dem das bilanzierende Unternehmen einen maßgeblichen Anteil von in der Regel mindestens 20% hält. Eine Kontrollmöglichkeit wird ausdrücklich nicht vorausgesetzt; wäre eine solche gegeben, läge der Fall eines verbundenen Unternehmens vor (s.o.). Die Bilanzen sonstiger Beteiligungsunternehmen werden daher auch nicht konsolidiert. Da die Beteiligung eines Unternehmens an einem anderen aber zweifellos ein für die Bilanzen maßgeblicher Umstand ist, muss dieses Ergebnis der Beteiligung in der Einnahme-Überschuss-Rechnung des die Anteile besitzenden Unternehmens erscheinen. Dies erfolgt anhand der „equity method of accounting" (FRS 2/SSAP 1), wonach im Wesentlichen der Anteil des besitzenden Unternehmens an dem Bilanzergebnis des Zielunternehmens Eingang in die Einnahme-Überschuss-Rechnung findet.

Umsatz aus anderen Investitionen

Alle Muster verlangen die gesonderte Angabe von Umsätzen aus anderen Investitionen jeglicher Art. Dies betrifft z.B. Dividendenzahlungen aus Beteiligungen an börsennotierten Gesellschaften. Auch diese müssen in der tatsächlich getätigten Höhe separat aufgeführt werden.

Umsatz aus Geschäftstätigkeit

Der operative Umsatz eines Unternehmens muss aufgeteilt werden in dauerhafte Geschäftsfelder (wiederum unterteilt in Akquisitionen und andere Umsätze, s. o.) und beendete Geschäftsfelder (s. o.). In der Regel wird unter dem Umsatz aus normaler Geschäftstätigkeit der Gesamtumsatz eines Unternehmens vor dessen Umsatz aus der Beteiligung an verbundenen Unternehmen definiert (s. o.).

SSAP 25 („segmental reporting") verlangt, den Umsatz aus jedem maßgeblichen Bereich der Geschäftstätigkeiten eines Unternehmens gesondert anzugeben.

Außergewöhnliche Posten

FRS 3 definiert außergewöhnliche Posten als solche Sachverhalte, die aus Ereignissen oder Transaktionen resultieren, welche zwar in den gewöhnlichen Geschäftsbereich des Unternehmens fallen, die jedoch in der Einnahme-Überschuss-

Rechnung und damit in der Bilanz des Unternehmens separat aufgeführt werden müssen, weil andernfalls aufgrund der Bedeutung der außergewöhnlichen Ereignisse eine wahrheitsgemäße Einschätzung der Gesamtlage des Unternehmens nicht möglich ist. Auch hier ist wiederum zwischen laufenden und beendeten Geschäftsvorfällen zu unterscheiden. Einzelheiten hierzu folgen später.

Schuldzinsen und vergleichbare Aufwendungen

Schuldzinsen und vergleichbare Aufwendungen sind in der Einnahme-Überschuss-Rechnung ebenfalls gesondert aufzuführen; dies betrifft insbesondere, aber nicht nur:

- Schuldzinsen für Darlehen
- Zinsbestandteile bei Finanzierungsleasing und Schuldverschreibungen
- Gebühren und Kosten im Zusammenhang mit Darlehen und Kreditverträgen

Darüber hinaus verlangt der Companies Act die Analyse der Darlehensverpflichtungen des Unternehmens für einen Zeitraum von fünf Jahren für alle Arten von Krediten und verwandten Geschäften, gleichgültig, ob Ratenkredit oder nicht.

Darüber hinaus besteht die Möglichkeit, Zinsen für Darlehen, mit denen feste Vermögenswerte geschaffen werden, zu kapitalisieren; hier sind die Einzelheiten freilich umstritten und schwierig und dürften für die meisten Fälle der zugezogenen Limited bedeutungslos sein.

Zahlreiche Unternehmen setzen von den Schuldzinsen die erzielten Zinsen ab. Dies ist grundsätzlich zulässig.

Gewinn oder Verlust vor Steuern

Der Gewinn oder Verlust eines Unternehmens aus gewöhnlicher Geschäftstätigkeit vor Steuern muss in der Einnahme-Überschuss-Rechnung als Kernangabe enthalten sein. Die Position erfasst auch außergewöhnliche Posten, sofern diese in Zusammenhang mit dem gewöhnlichen Geschäftsbetrieb des Unternehmens stehen. Ausgenommen sind lediglich Steuern und außergewöhnliche Ereignisse, die nicht in Zusammenhang mit dem gewöhnlichen Geschäftsverkehr des Unternehmens stehen (dazu gleich).

Steuern

Der Companies Act und SSAP 8 bzw. 15 verlangen, dass grundsätzlich die folgenden Angaben in Bezug auf die Unternehmenssteuern zu erfolgen haben:

1. Steuern auf Gewinn oder Verlust aus gewöhnlicher Geschäftstätigkeit
2. Steuern auf außerordentliche Gewinne oder Verluste
3. Andere von den Ziff. 1 und 2 nicht erfasste Steuern

zu Ziff. 1:

Die Angabe der Steuern auf Gewinn und Verlust aus gewöhnlicher Geschäftstätigkeit müssen folgendes berücksichtigen:

- Unternehmenssteuern im Vereinigten Königreich auf Gewinne im Berichtszeitraum
- Unter Doppelbesteuerungsabkommen fallende Steuern im Ausland

- später fällige Steuern
- ausländische Steuern
- Einkommenssteuern
- wesentliche Unterschiede zu vorausgegangenen Berichtsperioden

Der unbestimmte Begriff der später fälligen Steuern (latente Steuern, „deferred taxation") wird nicht einheitlich definiert. Üblicherweise werden hierunter erst später fällige Steuern verstanden, die ihren Ursprung aber in gegenwärtigen Geschäftsvorfällen haben. Dies kann z. B. der Fall sein, wenn die Einnahme-Überschuss-Rechnung aufgrund von abgerechneten Umsätzen, die Steuererklärungen aber aufgrund von tatsächlich vereinnahmten Entgelten erstellt wird.

Ausländische Steuern müssen in jedem Falls separat aufgeführt werden, gleichgültig, ob sie unter ein Doppelbesteuerungsabkommen fallen oder nicht.

Außerordentliche Vorfälle und Korrekturen vorhergehender Einnahme-Überschuss-Rechnungen

Außerordentliche Vorfälle im Berichtszeitraum sind gesondert in der Einnahme-Überschuss-Rechnung aufzuführen und zu bilanzieren. Was hierunter zu verstehen ist, bleibt angesichts der Unbestimmtheit dieses Begriffes unklar.

Entscheidend ist, dass ein Vorfall sich weit außerhalb der normalen Geschäftsfelder des Unternehmens abspielt und er nicht ohne weiteres planbar war. Auch mit seiner Wiederholung darf nicht gerechnet werden. Allein der Umstand, dass der Vorfall einen Bezug zu einer vorangegangenen Bilanzperiode hat, macht ihn noch nicht zu einem außerordentlichen Vorgang. Auch außergewöhnliche Geschäftsvorgänge, die sich jedoch im Rahmen des normalen Geschäftsverkehrs des Unternehmens abspielen, zählen nicht hierzu.

Aus dieser engen Definition folgt, dass es in der Praxis kaum Raum für die Anwendung dieser engen Ausnahmevorschrift gibt, zumal die Definition des gewöhnlichen Geschäftsverkehrs mittlerweile derartig weit ist, dass es kaum noch Vorfälle gibt, die nicht hierunter fallen.

Sofern in vorangegangenen Bilanzen oder Einnahme-Überschuss-Rechnungen insoweit fehlerhafte Einordnungen vorgenommen wurden, müssen diese korrigiert werden. Gleiches gilt, wenn die Grundsätze der Unternehmensbilanzierung in zulässiger Weise (s. o.) geändert werden. Um Verzerrungen durch unterschiedliche Einordnung von Bilanzpositionen zu vermeiden, ist mindestens auf die abweichende Praxis in geeigneter Form hinzuweisen, im Regelfall bietet sich aber der Weg über die Korrektur an. In dem Fall fordert FRS 3 die erneute korrigierte Darstellung der Vergleichszahlen für die vorausgegangene Periode sowie deren Erläuterungen und darüber hinaus die Korrektur der Eröffnungsbilanz der aktuellen Periode sowie die Anpassung der Rückstellungen.

Behandlung von Minderheitsanteilen bei Konsolidierung

Wenn ein beherrschendes Unternehmen weniger als 100% der Anteile eines Unternehmens hält, so existieren notwendigerweise Minderheitseigner. Dies ist dann von Bedeutung, wenn das herrschende Unternehmen konsolidiert, da dann der Gesamtumsatz, der Gesamtaufwand und das Gesamtergebnis zu 100% dem herrschenden Unternehmen zugerechnet werden, auch wenn sein Anteil geringer ist. Der auf die Minderheitseigner entfallende Anteil muss daher in der Einnahme-Überschuss-Rechnung gesondert als solcher ausgewiesen werden („Minority Interests"). Dies erfolgt im konsolidierten Gewinn- und Verlust-Konto nach dem Gruppen- Ergebnis aus gewöhnlicher Geschäftstätigkeit nach Steuern.

Gewinnausschüttungen

Der Companies Act verlangt die Angabe des Gesamtbetrages aller gezahlten und vorgeschlagenen Dividende in der Einnahme-Überschuss-Rechnung. Damit ist freilich noch nichts darüber gesagt, welche Gewinne überhaupt ausschüttungsfähig sind.

Grundlegend ist insoweit zunächst zwischen realisierten und nicht realisierten Umsätzen zu unterscheiden. Realisierte Gewinne sind solche, die im Einklang mit den anerkannten Bilanz- und Rechnungslegungsgrundsätzen als Ergebnis der aktuellen Einnahme-Überschuss-Rechnung erscheinen. Hieraus folgt, dass es in der Regel bei der Beurteilung dieser Frage keine Abweichungen zwischen der Einnahme-Überschuss-Rechnung bzw. der Bilanz und der Frage, in welcher Höhe Profite des Unternehmens ausschüttungsfähig sind, keine Abweichungen gibt. Hierbei gilt auch das bereits dargestellte Prinzip, wonach Gewinne erst mit deren Realisierung, Verluste hingegen bereits mit deren Entstehung bilanziert werden. Weiter gilt, dass zwar erwartete, aber noch nicht hinreichend sicher konkretisierte Gewinne nicht bilanziert werden dürfen und damit auch nicht ausschüttungsfähig sind.

Jedes Unternehmen, das Gewinne ausschütten möchte, muss solche zur freien Verfügung haben. Gewinne aus vergangenen Perioden, die nicht ausgeschüttet wurden, können in der aktuellen Periode ausgeschüttet werden. Vorgetragene Verluste aus vorangegangenen Perioden sind immer anzurechnen. Für börsennotierte Unternehmen gelten weitere Restriktionen, so dürfen sie nicht ausschütten, wenn nach der Ausschüttung die Summe des Stammkapitals und der nicht ausschüttungsfähigen Reserven angetastet wären. Nicht ausschüttungsfähige Reserven sind:

- share premium account

- Kapitaltilgungsreserve

- der übersteigende Betrag von addierten nicht realisierten Profiten mit der Summe nicht realisierter Verluste

- andere nicht ausschüttungsfähige Reserven (z.B. aufgrund der Regelungen in der Satzung der Gesellschaft)

Informationen über Mitarbeiter

In Bezug auf die Mitarbeiter muss die Bilanz immer die Gesamtanzahl der Mitarbeiter im Durchschnitt des laufenden Geschäftsjahres angegeben werden. Sofern die Umsätze nach Unternehmenssparten aufzuschlüsseln sind (s.o.), gilt das gleiche für die Mitarbeiterzahlen. Sofern der Durchschnitt der Mitarbeiterzahl im Berichtszeitraum stark und außergewöhnlich von der Mitarbeiterzahl zum Ende des Geschäftsjahres abweicht, etwa, weil Massenkündigungen ausgesprochen wurden, ist dies gesondert auszuweisen und zu erläutern.

Die Kosten für Mitarbeiter sind separat unter folgenden Rubriken aufzuführen:

- Löhne und Gehälter, gezahlt oder noch geschuldet
- Aufwendungen für soziale Sicherungssysteme, die das Unternehmen für die Mitarbeiter eingerichtet hat

Das Gesetz erlaubt ansonsten eine relativ große Flexibilität in Bezug auf die Art und Weise, wie diese Informationen präsentiert werden. Dies kann z.B. anhand der der Funktion der Mitarbeiter (Herstellung, Vertrieb, Verwaltung etc.) oder anhand der Spartenzugehörigkeit (PKW-Herstellung, Entwicklung, Vertrieb etc.) geschehen.

Zwingend vorgesehen ist jedoch immer die Angabe des Aufwandes für sämtliche nicht-staatlichen Altersvorsorgemaßnahmen des Unternehmens für seine Mitarbeiter. Hintergrund sind mögliche schwer kalkulierbare und oftmals auch hohe finanzielle Risiken, die sich für die Unternehmen aus dieser Form der Mitarbeiter-Entlohnung in der Zukunft ergeben können. Auf die typische „Limited" in Deutschland dürfte das freilich nicht zutreffen. In einfachen Fällen genügt ohnehin die Angabe der Pensionskosten im Berichtszeitraum sowie die Angabe etwaiger offener Beiträge bzw. von Vorauszahlungen.

Zuwendungen an die Geschäftsführung

Der Companies Act verlangt die gesonderte Angabe aller Zuwendungen an die Geschäftsführung des Unternehmens, sofern diese über 5.000 £ im Berichtszeitraum liegen. Folgende Zuwendungen fallen unter diese Regelung:

- Gehaltszahlungen, Prämien, Boni, Tantiemen, geldwerte Vorteile (etwa für die Nutzung von Firmenwagen) etc.
- Vorteile, die aus der Ausübung von Aktienoptionen erwachsen sind
- langfristige Zusagen, z.B. Pensionspläne, betriebliche Altersversorgung etc.
- Abfindungen
- Zahlungen an Dritte für die Geschäftsführung (z.B. Übernahme von Bankspesen)

Generell gilt, dass die Unternehmen umso detailliertere Angaben machen, je größer das Unternehmen ist und je höher und damit in der Regel auch fast immer aufwendiger die Zahlungen an die Geschäftsführung sind.

Vergleichszahlen

Die Präsentation von Vergleichszahlen aller maßgeblichen Größen in der Einnahme-Überschuss-Rechnung und in der Bilanz aus der vorausgegangenen Berichtsperiode ist zwingend erforderlich, um die Entwicklung des Unternehmens in allen wesentlichen Bereichen übersichtlich zu dokumentieren.

Einnahmen je Geschäftsanteil

Die Pflicht, die Einnahmen je Anteil am Unternehmen aufzulisten, betrifft nur börsennotierte Unternehmen und damit nicht die Limited.

Ausnahmen und Besonderheiten

Seit 1985 ist es gestattet, dass kleinere Unternehmen, die bestimmte Voraussetzungen erfüllen, lediglich reduzierte Einnahme-Überschuss-Rechnungen bzw. Bilanzen vorzulegen haben. Diese in der Praxis sehr wichtige Erleichterung gilt per Gesetz unabhängig davon, ob man sie beantragt hat, für alle Unternehmen, die unter die entsprechenden Tatbestände fallen.

Allerdings betreffen diese Erleichterungen ausschließlich diejenigen Dokumente, die dem Register vorzulegen und zu veröffentlichen sind. Berichtspflichten innerhalb des Unternehmens - etwa gegenüber Gesellschaftern - bleiben hiervon unberührt. Gleichwohl ist diese Erleichterung in der Praxis der Limited - und hier insbesondere der regelmäßig kleinen und von der Gesellschafterstruktur her zumeist unkomplizierten, einfach strukturierten Limited im Auslandseinsatz - von außerordentlich großer Bedeutung.

Grundsätzlich muss es sich bei den begünstigten Unternehmen um **kleine oder mittlere Unternehmen** handeln. Hierunter fallen generell **nicht**:

- Börsennotierte Unternehmen oder von börsennotierten Unternehmen abhängige Unternehmen
- Banken und Versicherungen und alle mit ihnen verbundenen Unternehmen

Für alle anderen Unternehmen gilt:

Ein **mittleres Unternehmen** liegt vor, wenn

- der Umsatz 11,2 Mio. £ nicht überschritten hat
- die Bilanzsumme 5,6 Mio. £ nicht überschritten hat

- die durchschnittliche Zahl der Arbeitnehmer 250 je Arbeitswoche nicht überschritten hat

Ein **kleines Unternehmen** liegt vor, wenn

- der Umsatz 2,8 Mio. £ nicht überschritten hat
- die Bilanzsumme 1,4 Mio. £ nicht überschritten hat
- die durchschnittliche Zahl der Arbeitnehmer 50 je Arbeitswoche nicht überschritten hat

Als Bilanzsumme gilt dabei die Summe aller Vermögenswerte wie in der Bilanz ausgeworfen, ohne Abzug von Verbindlichkeiten. Welche Erleichterungen im einzelnen gelten, hängen von der Einordnung des Unternehmens ab.

Ausnahmen für mittlere Unternehmen

Mittlere Unternehmen können folgende Angaben unterlassen: Umsatz, Vertriebskosten, sonstige Umsätze, Analyse von Umsätzen und Kosten nach den jeweiligen Geschäftsbereichen und eine Analyse der Umsatze nach den jeweiligen Märkten, auf denen das Unternehmen tätig ist. Im Übrigen gilt, dass die gesamte Einnahme-Überschuss-Rechnung, Bilanz und die Erläuterungen - beschränkt auf die o. g. Angaben - so zu erstellen ist, wie dies bereits dargestellt wurde. Die Ausnahmen für mittlere Unternehmen sind daher in der Praxis wenig bedeutsam.

Ausnahmen für kleine Unternehmen

Im Gegensatz hierzu bestehen weite Ausnahmen für kleine Unternehmen. Sie brauchen die folgenden Unterlagen nicht zwingend einzureichen:

- Einnahme-Überschuss-Rechnung
- Unternehmensbericht
- Angaben zu Zuwendungen an Geschäftsführer und leitende Angestellte
- Alle Angaben, die im folgenden Kapitel (Bilanz) mit römischen Zahlen versehen sind
- Weite Teile der ansonsten erforderlichen Berichtspflicht (dazu später)

Bei diesen weitgehenden Ausnahmen darf freilich nicht übersehen werden, dass auch für kleine Unternehmen der Grundsatz der vollständigen und wahrheitsgemäßen Bilanzierung gilt. Diese Ausnahmen betreffen in erster Linie die Frage, welche Informationen ein Unternehmen beim Handelsregister einreichen muss und nicht die Frage, wie die Bilanzen und die Einnahme-Überschuss-Rechnungen gestaltet werden müssen. Hier können sich im Einzelfall unter anderem aus Satzungsbestimmungen weitergehende Erfordernisse ableiten. Für die einfache Limited im Auslandseinsatz dürfte das aber nur selten zutreffen. Hier bleibt es bei den weitreichenden Liberalisierungen für kleine Unternehmen in Bezug auf die Rechnungslegung.

DIE HANDELSBILANZ

Die Handelsbilanz spiegelt die finanzielle Position eines Unternehmens an einen bestimmten Stichtag wieder. Die Handelsbilanz gibt in der Regel Detailinformationen über die Vermögenswerte des Unternehmens, seine Verbindlichkeiten und deren Natur und ermöglicht daher eine genaue Bewertung des Unternehmens.

In diesem Kapitel werden die verschiedenen Format vorgestellt, die unter dem Companies Act (1985) für die Abfassung von Bilanzen gewählt werden können, erläutert die einzelnen Bestandteile der Bilanz und in den Erläuterungen und beschäftigt sich darüber hinaus mit weiteren Fragen, die bei der Erstellung der Bilanz von Bedeutung sind.

Zur Verfügung stehende Muster

Es gibt zwei für die Handelsbilanz zugelassene Muster. Grob unterscheiden sich beide Vorlagen durch ihre Gliederung. Die erste Vorlage ist vertikal gegliedert und wird von den meisten Unternehmen verwendet. Sie hat sich insbesondere bei kleineren und mittleren Unternehmen in der Praxis durchgesetzt. Das zweite Format ist horizontal gegliedert und findet in erster Linie bei komplexeren Bilanzen Anwendung, wenngleich die Wahl grundsätzlich freigestellt ist.

Wichtig ist, dass die vorgegebenen römischen Gliederungspunkte bis ins Detail (also z.B. auch die Gliederungsnummerierung!) einzuhalten ist, in diesem Punkt werden keine Ausnahmen geduldet. In Bezug auf die (arabischen) Untergliederungspunkte wird eine größere Flexibilität gewährt. Sie können bei Bedarf den Besonderheiten des bilanzierenden Unternehmens angepasst werden. In jedem Fall muss jede Abweichung von den Vorgaben dargestellt und begründet werden, und zwar in den Erläuterungen zur Bilanz.

Im Folgenden werden die einzelnen Positionen dargestellt und erläutert. Es ist dabei sinnvoll, die jeweiligen Muster (Anhang) vorzuhalten.

Allgemeine Bewertungsgrundsätze

Der 4. Anhang zum Companies Act 1985 (in der heute geltenden Fassung) enthält einige Regelungen für die Bewertung von Bilanzansätzen. Hier werden zunächst nur die generellen Bewertungsgrundsätze dargelegt, später (bei der Behandlung der einzelnen Vermögensgegenstände) werden diese dann im Einzelnen behandelt.

Grundsätzlich existieren mehrere im Prinzip gleichwertige Bewertungsgrundsätze nebeneinander. So kann man auf den Anschaffungspreis oder die Produktionskosten eines Vermögensgegenstandes abstellen, auf den aktuellen Marktwert oder (z.B. für Lagerbestände) auf den aktuellen Einkaufswert. Welchen Grundsatz man wo anwendet, richtet sich nach den Besonderheiten des Einzelfalles.

Laufende Abschreibungen sind überall dort vorzunehmen, wo nach dem gewöhnlichen Geschäftsverlauf mit einem regelmäßigen Wertverlust zu rechnen hat. Dies gilt z.B. für Fahrzeuge und Maschinen. Sofern Investitionen betroffen sind, können Abschreibungen auch dann vorgenommen werden, wenn dauerhafte und langfristige Wertminderungen nicht zu erwarten sind. Vermögensgegenstände mit klar begrenzter Lebensdauer können nach bestimmten Raten fest abgeschrieben werden, genaueres hierzu wird später erläutert. Das Umlaufvermögen soll auf den Betrag des aktuellen Wiederverkaufswertes abgeschrieben werden, es sei denn, die Einstandkosten oder eine andere akzeptierte Bewertungsmethode führen zu geringeren Ansätzen. Genaueres auch dazu später.

Werden einmal vorgenommene Abschreibungen durch spätere Ereignisse wieder aufgehoben, etwa durch marktbedingte unvorhersehbare Wertsteigerungen, so sind die Abschreibungen im Rahmen der Einnahme-Überschuss-Rechnung wieder zu korrigieren.

Current Cost Accounting

Die Verpflichtung, ein current cost accounting aufzustellen hat zum Ziel, sicherzustellen, dass das Betriebsvermögen des Unternehmens in der Bilanz möglichst genau den tatsächlichen und aktuellen Marktwerten der Einzelpositionen entspricht. Dies ist auch im Interesse der Unternehmen, da etwa im Falle steigender Preise eine Anpassung der Bilanzwerte an diese aktuellen Preise die Eigenkapitalausstattung des Unternehmens erhöht. Der aktuelle Anschaffungs- oder Verkaufswert eines Vermögensbestandteils wird - vereinfacht dargestellt - definiert als Differenz zwischen seinem Wiederbeschaffungswert und seinem Verkaufswert, wobei die Berechnung im Einzelfall kompliziert sein kann.

Neubewertung von Vermögenswerten

Sobald Vermögensbestandteile neu bewertet werden, entsteht zwangsläufig ein Gewinn oder ein Verlust aus diesem Vorgang. Hierfür gibt es in der Bilanz eine spezielle Rückstellungs-Position („valuation reserve"). Wird z.B. ein Grundstück mit einem Buchwert von 400.000 £ aufgrund der veränderten Marktlage mit 500.000 £ bewertet, entsteht ein Gewinn in Höhe der Differenz von 100.000 £, der nicht in der Einnahme-Überschuss-Rechnung aufscheint, sondern nur in der Bilanzposition für Rückstellungen aus Neubewertungen von Vermögensgegenständen. Der Gewinn von 100.000 £ würde aber Bestandteil des in der Bilanz ausgewiesenen Gesamtgewinns des Unternehmens erscheinen (siehe dazu im Einzelnen Kapitel 5). Würde das Grundstück später für 550.000 £ verkauft werden, so würde die Rückstellungsposition aufgelöst und der Gewinn als realisierter Gewinn in die Einnahme-Überschuss-Rechnung transferiert. In diesem Fall würde der Gewinn 50.000 £ betragen, nämlich die Differenz zwischen dem Erlös (550.000 £) und dem Buchwert einschließlich Reserven (500.000 £). Etwaige Abschreibungsbeträge sind hiervon unberührt.

In der Praxis verwenden in dem Vereinigten Königreich nur wenige Unternehmen in ihren Bilanzen das historische Kosten-Prinzip und noch weniger verwenden durchgängig das Prinzip der aktuellen Kosten. Ersteres ist oftmals zu ungenau, letzteres würde zu häufige Aktualisierungen erfordern. In der Praxis wird in aller Regel eine Mixtur aus allen zulässigen Verfahren angewendet. So hat sich eingebürgert, für bestimmte Vermögenswerte die (ggf. fortgeschriebenen) Anschaffungskosten anzusetzen, für andere aber (z.B. für Lagerbestände) die tatsächlichen aktuellen Kosten. Dennoch ist in diesem Punkt keine wirklich einheitliche Praxis zu beobachten. Im Rahmen der zulässigen Bewertungsverfahren können Unternehmen frei wählen und sind auch nicht dazu verpflichtet, etwa ihre Wahl zu begründen oder aber den sich möglicherweise ändernden üblichen Gepflogenheiten anzupassen. Das führt naturgemäß zu einer nur eingeschränkten Vergleichbarkeit verschiedener Bilanzen. Aus diesem Grund sind Unternehmen, die allein auf Basis der Anschaffungskosten bilanzieren, verpflichtet, hierauf gesondert hinzuweisen (FRS 3). Das ASB vertritt darüber hinaus die Auffassung, dass eine Rückkehr zum vollständigen Prinzip der Anschaffungskosten nicht akzeptabel sei, da hierdurch fast immer das Prinzip der Wirklichkeitsnähe der Bilanzen verletzt werde. Dies ist angesichts des tatsächlichen Wertkorrekturbedarfes auch kaum von der Hand zu weisen.

Inhalt der Bilanz

Anlagevermögen (fixed assets)

Der Companies Act definiert das Anlagevermögen eines Unternehmens als das Vermögen, welches auf dauerhafter Basis für die Geschäftstätigkeit des Unternehmens verwendet wird. Andere Vermögenswerte müssen im Umlaufvermögen aufgeführt werden. Das Anlagevermögen muss mindestens in folgende Kategorien unterteilt werden:

- Immaterielles Anlagevermögen
- Sachanlagevermögen
- Investitionen in das Anlagevermögen

Darüber hinaus ist es erforderlich, in den Erläuterungen zur Bilanz für jeden Gegenstand des Anlagevermögens Angaben zu machen über die Kosten (oder die korrigierten Kosten) zu Beginn und zum Ende der Finanzperiode. Gleiches gilt für den Einfluss, den jeder Gegenstand des Anlagevermögens auf Anschaffungen, Verfügungen oder Verkäufe des Unternehmens hatte. Sofern gegenüber früheren Berichtszeiträumen die Bilanzierungsmethode oder Bewertungsmethode verändert wurde, ist auch dies zu erläutern.

Wurden im Berichtszeitraum Abschreibungen oder Rückstellungen im Hinblick auf einzelne Gegenstände des Anlagevermögens gemacht, so müssen auch diese gesondert erläutert werden. Gleiches gilt naturgemäß auch für die Erläuterung der gewählten Methode zur Berechnung der Abschreibung des Anlagevermögens (siehe dazu im Einzelnen oben) ebenso wie für die Angabe der wesentlichen Faktoren für die Berechnung (z.B. zugrunde gelegte Lebensdauer des Anlagegegenstands).

Immaterielle Vermögenswerte (intangible assets)

Auch immaterielle Vermögenswerte müssen in der Bilanz aufgelistet werden, und zwar unter der entsprechenden, zwingend vorgegebenen Überschrift. Die Angaben sind zu untergliedern in:

- Entwicklungskosten
- Patente, Lizenzen und vergleichbare Rechte
- Goodwill
- Akontozahlungen

Nach dem Gesetz dürfen lediglich in Ausnahmesituationen Positionen als „Entwicklungskosten" verbucht werden, wobei unklar ist, wann eine solche Ausnahmesituation vorliegt. Grundsätzlich dürfen Aufwendung für Forschung und Entwicklung nicht kapitalisiert werden, so dass ein besonderer Grund vorliegen muss, der dies ausnahmsweise rechtfertigen kann. Ein solcher Grund kann z.B. darin liegen, dass diese Kosten eindeutig und unzweifelhaft einem konkreten, abgrenzbaren Projekt zuzuordnen sind, dass die Resultate dieses konkreten Projektes mit hoher Wahrscheinlichkeit vom Unternehmen kommerziell erfolgreich verwertet werden können, dass die späteren Erträge die Entwicklungskosten wahrscheinlich deutlich übersteigen werden und dass hinreichende Ressourcen (insbesondere Finanzkraft) des Unternehmens vorhanden sind, um das Projekt erfolgreich zu Ende zu führen.

Der Begriff „Goodwill" wird nicht im Gesetz definiert, doch gemeinhin wird hierunter die Differenz des Wertes eines Unternehmens als Ganzes und der Summe seines Nettovermögens angesehen (vgl. SSAP 22). Die Bilanzierung des Goodwills in der Bilanz ist regelmäßig nur dann statthaft, wenn es sich um hinzu gekauften Goodwill handelt, für den das Unternehmen selber in nachvollziehbarer Weise eine Gegenleistung erbracht hat. Die Bilanzierung des durch unternehmensinterne Maßnahmen geschaffenen Goodwills ist daher nicht zulässig. Hintergrund ist, die Bewertung bilanzierten Goodwills objektiv nachvollziehbar zu gestalten und Bilanzmanipulationen durch den Einsatz objektiv nicht nachvollziehbarer Werte in jedem Fall zu unterbinden. Anders sieht die Situation aus, wenn ein Unternehmen ein anderes kauft und hierbei ein Teil des Kaufpreises für den goodwill gezahlt wird. Dieser Bestandteil muss bilanziert werden.

In aller Regel wird in solch einem Fall der Wert des gekauften goodwills unverzüglich abgeschrieben und mit den Rückstellungen verrechnet. Die in vielen anderen Ländern übliche Praxis, den goodwill über seine voraussichtliche „Lebensdauer" abzuschreiben, wird im Vereinigten Königreich nur ausnahmsweise praktiziert. Seit 1998 freilich wird auch diese Variante vermehrt angewendet, allerdings mit der Maßgabe, dass der Abschreibungszeitraum in aller Regel 20 Jahre nicht überschreiten soll.

Markennamen und andere immaterielle Vermögenswerte vergleichbarer Art (Patente, Warenzeichen etc.) werden oftmals im Rahmen des goodwills mit erfasst und bilanztechnisch behandelt. In den meisten Fällen genügt dies auch, Ausnahmen sind unter Geltung des Grundsatzes der Wahrheit der Bilanzen nur dann geboten, wenn der Markenname oder der immaterielle Vermögenswert eine derart herausgehobene Bedeutung hat, dass seine gesonderte Bilanzierung angezeigt erscheint. Im Fall der kleineren „Limited" wird dies aber kaum jemals der Fall sein.

Sachanlagen (tangible assets)

Sachanlagen müssen in der Bilanz aufgelistet werden, und zwar unter der entsprechenden, zwingend vorgegebenen Überschrift. Die Angaben sind zu untergliedern in:

- Grundstücke und Gebäude
- Werksanlagen und Maschinenpark

- Werkzeuge, sonstige Ausrüstung, unbewegliches Inventar, Zubehör
- Akontozahlungen und unfertige Sachanlagen

Die Kategorie „Grundstücke und Gebäude" muss unterteilt werden nach Eigentum und gemieteten Immobilien. Bei Mietverträgen wird unterschieden zwischen lang- und kurzfristigen Verträgen. Langfristigkeit liegt vor, wenn die voraussichtliche zukünftige Nutzungsdauer der Immobilie mindestens 50 Jahre beträgt.

Neben dem reinen Wert der Immobilien sind deren Nebenkosten wie z.B. Erwerbskosten (Notar, Makler, Aufbereitungskosten, Abrisskosten etc.) an dieser Stelle in der Bilanz anzusetzen. Auch Aufwendungen für Reparaturen und Werterhalt gehören hierher; gleiches gilt für immobilienbezogene Verwaltungskosten (Hausmeister, Wohnungsverwaltung etc.).

Auch bei anderen Gegenständen des Sachanlagevermögens ist nicht nur deren Wert, sondern auch alle hiermit verbunden Aufwendungen und Kosten (Frachtkosten, Zoll, Aufstellkosten etc.) in Ansatz zu bringen.

Sofern Zinsaufwendungen für Sachanlagevermögen kapitalisiert und an dieser Stelle in Ansatz gebracht werden, so muss in den Anmerkungen der Bilanz ein Hinweis auf diesen Umstand erfolgen.

Gemietete Vermögensgegenstände (Leased assets)

Grundsätzlich hat die Bilanz eines Unternehmens nach SSAP 21 sämtliche Einflüsse von Miet- und Pachtverträgen auf dessen Finanzstatus vollständig und korrekt wiederzugeben.

Die Behandlung im Rahmen der Buchführung unterscheidet danach, ob es sich bei den Miet- und Pachtverträgen um Finanzierungs-Leasing oder operative Miete handelt. Finanzierungs-Leasing liegt nach SSAP 21 immer dann vor, wenn der Mieter nach Gesamtbetrachtung der Sachlage das typische wirtschaftliche Risiko des Eigentümers trägt (z. B. „Sale and lease back"). Liegt ein Fall des Finanzierungs-Leasings vor, so ist der betreffende Vermögenswert so zu bilanzieren, als würde das Unternehmen ihn zu Eigentum besitzen. Im Fall des Finanzierungs-Leasing betrifft ein solcher Vertrag die Bilanz an verschiedenen Stellen: Einmal wird der geleaste Gegenstand des Anlagevermögens herkömmlich wie Eigentum als Sachanlagevermögen bilanziert, zum anderen erscheint die Verpflichtung zu Zahlung des Mietzinses bei den Verbindlichkeiten. Von Bedeutung ist ferner, dass der Abschreibungszeitraum in aller Regel nicht länger als die Restlaufzeit des Leasing-Vertrages gewählt werden darf, jedenfalls dann nicht, wenn der Vermögensgegenstand nach Ablauf des Leasingvertrages an den Leasinggeber zurückzugeben ist. Außerdem sollte der Wert des Leasinggegenstandes die Mindestsumme aller zu zahlenden Leasingraten einschließlich etwaiger Sonderzahlungen nicht unterschreiten.

An dieser Stelle wird im Übrigen das Prinzip der inhaltlichen Wahrheit von Bilanzen und sein Vorrang vor formalen Aspekten deutlich: Unter den dargestellten Voraussetzungen sind gemietete Vermögenswerte wie Eigentum zu bilanzieren, obgleich sie formaljuristisch nicht im Eigentum des Unternehmens stehen.

Die Einzelheiten der Bilanzierung komplexer Finanzierungs-Leasing-Verträge sind kompliziert und detailreich, sofern solche bilanziert werden müssen, muss der Unternehmer immer auf die Hilfe englischer Steuerberater zurückgreifen.

Investitionen (Investments)

Unter der Ägide der beiden zulässigen Bilanz-Formate werden Investitionen eines Unternehmens entweder - abhängig von ihrem Charakter - im Umlauf- oder Anlagevermögen bilanziert. Folgende Informationen sind immer gesondert auszuweisen:

- Erwerb von Anteilen an verbundenen Unternehmen
- Darlehen an verbundene Unternehmen
- Erwerb maßgeblichen (bestimmenden) Einflusses auf ein anderes Unternehmen
- Darlehen an Unternehmen, auf die ein bestimmender Einfluss besteht
- Andere Investitionen (Nicht-Darlehen)
- Andere Darlehen
- Erwerb eigener Anteile

Grundsätzlich ist dabei immer zwischen Anteilen an börsennotierten Unternehmen und anderen zu unterscheiden, da der Wert der ersteren oftmals größeren Schwankungen unterliegt.

Sobald der Anteil an einem anderen Unternehmen - gleich welcher Art - 10% überschreitet oder die Investition 10% des Vermögens des anderen Unternehmens übersteigt, müssen darüber hinaus folgende weitere Angaben gemacht werden:

- Name des anderen Unternehmens
- Heimatland und Register des anderen Unternehmens
- Genaue Angaben zur Art der Beteiligung

Börsennotierte Unternehmen müssen noch weitere Angaben machen, z.B. zum regionalen und sachlichen Hauptbetätigungsfeld des Beteiligungsunternehmens.

Umlaufvermögen (Current Assets)

Lagerbestände müssen zwingend als solche und unter dieser Bezeichnung in der Bilanz aufgeführt werden. Der Lagerbestand ist wie folgt aufzuteilen:

- Roh- und Verbrauchsmaterial
- Unfertige Arbeiten
- verkaufsfertiger Lagerbestand
- Vorschusszahlungen

In Sonderfällen, wenn der Grundsatz der Wahrheit und Klarheit von Bilanzen dies fordert, kann von diesen Vorgaben auch abgewichen werden, allerdings sollte dies dann gesondert begründet werden. SSAP 9 verlangt, dass die Grundsätze der Bilanzierung von Lagerbeständen und unfertigen arbeiten dokumentiert werden muss. Je weiter sich das Unternehmen dabei von den üblichen Regularien entfernt, desto weiter geht naturgemäß diese Begründungs- und Erläuterungspflicht. Der Wertansatz von Lagerbeständen bzw. unfertigen arbeiten bestimmt sich nach dem Anschaffungspreis oder den Herstellungskosten; sollte der Verkaufswert jedoch geringer sein, ist dieser anzusetzen.

Forderungen (Deptors)

Sämtliche Forderungen des Unternehmens müssen in der Bilanz ausgewiesen werden, und zwar unterteilt nach

- Forderungen aus laufender Geschäftstätigkeit
- Forderungen an verbundene Unternehmen
- Forderungen an Unternehmen, an denen eine Beteiligung besteht
- Andere Forderungen
- Gezeichnetes, aber noch nicht eingezahltes Kapital
- Geleistete Vorauszahlungen

Die Position „Forderungen aus laufender Geschäftstätigkeit" enthält unter anderem Forderungen an Kunden und Forderungen an Lieferanten.

Unter die Position „andere Forderungen" fallen alle diejenigen Positionen, die nicht aus laufender Geschäftstätigkeit des Unternehmens resultieren und die keiner anderen Rubrik zuzuordnen sind. Hier ist weiter nach folgenden Kriterien aufzuschlüsseln:

- Darlehen an leitende Angestellte
- Darlehen an Geschäftsführer
- Darlehen an finance share purchases

Die Positionen „gezeichnetes Kapital" und „Vorauszahlungen" können unter „andere Forderungen" verbucht werden, wenn ihre Höhe unerheblich ist.

Kassenbestand und Bankkonto

Dieser Bilanzposten erfasst den gesamten Barbestand des Unternehmens ebenso wie alle kurzfristig verfügbaren Beträge und Verbindlichkeiten (z.B. Überziehungskredit, aber nur, soweit tatsächlich in Anspruch genommen), sowie andere Surrogate für Bargeld (z.B. Schecks, die eingereicht, aber noch nicht gutgeschrieben wurden).

Verbindlichkeiten (Creditors)

Verbindlichkeiten sind nach ihrer Laufzeit aufzuteilen. Kurzfristige Verbindlichkeiten sind danach solche, die innerhalb eines Jahres fällig werden, langfristige solche, die später zur Rückzahlung fällig werden. Bei Ratenkrediten ist der Zeitpunkt der letzten Rate entscheidend.

Darüber hinaus verlangt der Companies Act die folgende Differenzierung, und zwar entweder in der Bilanz selber oder in den Erläuterungen:

- Schuldverschreibungen
- Bankkredite und Überziehungskredite
- erhaltene Vorschusszahlungen für noch nicht erbrachte Leistungen
- Verbindlichkeiten gegenüber Handelspartnern und Lieferanten

- fällige Wechselverbindlichkeiten
- Verbindlichkeiten gegenüber verbundenen Unternehmen
- Verbindlichkeiten gegenüber an Unternehmen, an denen eine maßgebliche Beteiligung besteht
- Andere Verbindlichkeiten einschließlich Steuern und Sozialversicherungskosten
- accruals and deferred income

In aller Regel muss diese Klassifikation eingehalten werden, allein dort, wo einzelne dieser Positionen in Ausnahmefällen nur eine vollkommen untergeordnete Bedeutung zukommt, können sie unter der Position „andere Verbindlichkeiten" aufgeführt werden. Im Zweifel ist jedoch immer die vorgeschriebene Klassifikation zu beachten.

Verwirrend ist unter Umständen die Aufteilung von Steuerschulden unter die Rubriken „Andere Verbindlichkeiten einschließlich Steuern" und „Rückstellungen für Steuern" (dazu gleich). Für langfristige Verbindlichkeiten (das sind solche, deren Laufzeit noch mindestens 5 Jahre nach dem Datum der Bilanz beträgt), müssen außerdem folgende Angaben gemacht werden:

- Der gesamte zurückzuzahlende Betrag
- Die Gesamtsumme der Teilzahlungsbeträge innerhalb der nächsten fünf Jahre sowie der auf den späteren Zeitraum entfallenden Gesamtbetrag
- eine Darstellung der Fälligkeitstermine
- Die Zahlungsbedingungen, insbesondere die vereinbarten Zinsen und Sonderzahlungen

Umwandelbare Verbindlichkeiten (z.B. Darlehensverbindlichkeiten, die vertraglich nach Wahl des Darlehensgebers auch durch eine Beteiligung am Kapital des Unternehmens getilgt werden können) sind ebenfalls und ausnahmslos unter dem Bilanzposten „Verbindlichkeiten" aufzuführen.

Rückstellungen für Gewährleistung und Verbindlichkeiten

Rückstellungen für Gewährleistung und Verbindlichkeiten müssen generell unter einer gesonderten Rubrik in der Bilanz aufgeführt werden. Dabei müssen die Angaben in folgende Unter-Rubriken unterteilt werden:

- Rückstellungen für Pensionen und vergleichbare Verbindlichkeiten
- Rückstellungen für Steuerverbindlichkeiten, einschließlich Ratenverbindlichkeiten
- Andere Rückstellungen

Rückstellungen sind immer dann zu bilden, wenn Verbindlichkeiten nach vernünftiger kaufmännischer Einschätzung drohen, ihr Eintritt der Höhe und den Zeitpunkt nach aber ungewiss ist *(„Any amount retained as reasonably necessary for the purpose of providing for any liability or loss which is either likely to be incurred but uncertain as to amount or as to date on which it will arise")*.

Kapital und Reserven

Auch in Bezug auf das Kapital und auf die Reserven des Unternehmens stellt der Companies Act 1985 (in der geltenden

Fassung) strenge Offenlegungskriterien in der Bilanz auf. Danach müssen angegeben werden:

- Die Summe des nominellen Kapitals
- Die Summe des gezeichneten Kapitals
- Die Summe des eingezahlten Kapitals
- Rückstände in Bezug auf die Verpflichtung zur Zahlung von Dividenden

Bei größeren Unternehmen sind darüber hinaus Angaben zu verschiedenen Gruppen von Anteilseignern mit unterschiedlichen Rechten etc. zu machen, dies dürfte für eine kleine Standard-Limited im Auslandseinsatz freilich so gut wie nie zutreffen.

Sonstige Reserven

Hier kommen insbesondere Reserven aus Kapitalerhöhungsmaßnahmen bzw. aus dem Erwerb eigener Anteile in Betracht. Dies muss ggf. in der Bilanz angegeben werden.

Interessen von Minderheitsbeteiligten

Auch dieser Bilanzposten trifft auf kleinere Limiteds in aller Regel nicht zu. Er ist vielmehr für Publikumsgesellschaften mit Streubesitz vorgesehen.

Eventualverbindlichkeiten und Verpflichtungen

Eventualverbindlichkeiten

Hierunter versteht man Sachverhalte, deren Entstehung zum Zeitpunkt der Bilanzierung zwar nach wahrscheinlich, deren Ergebnis und vor allem deren Zeitpunkt aber noch offen ist. Entscheidend ist die „Wahrscheinlichkeit" nach vernünftigen kaufmännischen Maßstäben (SSAP 18). Dies gilt zum Beispiel für etwaige Verpflichtungen aus Rechtsstreitigkeiten, Garantieversprechen, unklaren Steuerverbindlichkeiten und ähnlichen Positionen. Es genügt, den voraussichtlichen Betrag der Aufwendung und den voraussichtlichen Entstehungszeitraum anzugeben. In aller Regel ist keine exakte Erläuterung dieser Position erforderlich, es sei denn, ihr Betrag ist im Verhältnis zur Bilanzsumme bedeutend.

Verpflichtungen

Das Gesetz verlangt immer die Angabe folgender Verpflichtungsgeschäfte nach der folgenden Gliederung:

- Kapitalverpflichtungen (die vertragliche Verpflichtung zur zukünftigen Leistung ist bereits eingegangen)

- Pensionsverpflichtungen und vergleichbare Verpflichtungen

- sonstige Verpflichtungen, deren Realisierung nach vernünftigen kaufmännischen Maßstäben hinreichend wahrscheinlich erscheint

Generell gilt auch hier wieder der Grundsatz, dass die Bilanz den tatsächlichen Finanzstatus des Unternehmens widerspiegeln muss. Sofern für dessen realistische Einschätzung die Darstellung von zukünftigen Verpflichtungsgeschäften erforderlich ist, sind diese aufzuführen.

Ereignisse nach Bilanzerstellung

Grundsätzlich hat die Bilanz alle Ereignisse zu erfassen, die sich auf den Bilanzzeitraum (siehe oben) erstrecken. Ereignisse, die später geschehen, sind in der späteren Bilanz zu berücksichtigen. Eine Ausnahme von diesem Grundsatz bilden Ereignisse, die sich nach Erstellung der Bilanz, aber vor deren Unterzeichnung ereignen und die eine Auswirkung auf den laufenden Bilanzierungszeitraum haben. In diesem Fall wird wie folgt verfahren:

- Ereignisse, die eine Korrektur der Bilanz bedürfen, weil Bilanzpositionen infolge der späteren Ereignisse verändert sind, sind z.B. die Insolvenz eines Gesellschaftsschuldners, der generelle Verfall der Verkaufspreise eines Produktes des Unternehmens, der dazu führt, dass der Wert des Lagerbestandes drastisch nach unten zu korrigieren ist oder die Entdeckung von Fehlern in der bisherigen Bilanz.
- Ereignisse, die nicht zwingend der Korrektur der bereits aufgestellten, aber noch nicht unterzeichneten Bilanz bedürfen, sind z.B. der allgemeine Wertverlust von Gegenständen des Anlagevermögens, die Neubewertung von Forderungen z.B. infolge veränderter Wechselkurse oder der Zukauf von Geschäftsbereichen. Letztere bedürfen keiner nach-

träglichen Bilanzkorrektur, sind aber in aller Regel in den Erläuterungen zu erwähnen.

Genaueres regelt SSAP 17 („Accounting for post balance sheets events"). Darüber hinaus verlangt der Companies Act, dass jedenfalls der Bericht der Geschäftsführung ("Directors Report") alle wesentlichen Informationen zu nachträglichen relevanten Ereignissen enthält, auch wenn diese nicht zwingend zu einer Bilanzkorrektur führen.

Da die Abgrenzung zwischen korrekturpflichtigen und nicht korrekturpflichtigen Ereignissen schwierig ist und im Einzelfall einen weiten Beurteilungsspielraum eröffnen kann, ist es sinnvoll, die Kriterien, die zu der konkreten Einordnung geführt haben, in den Anmerkungen zur Bilanz festzuhalten.

Cash flow statement

Seit 1991 müssen Unternehmen in ihren Bilanzen sog. cash-flow-statements abgeben, aus denen sich die Liquiditätslagfe des Unternehmens besser einschätzen lässt (FRS 1). Allerdings sind kleine Unternehmen hiervon nicht betroffen, so dass der Regelfall der Limited im Auslandseinsatz von diesem komplizierten und in der Praxis nicht immer einfach zu erfüllenden Erfordernis befreit ist.

Andere Erklärungen und Berichte

Erklärung über die gesamten Gewinne und Verluste

Diese Erklärung wird dem Umstand gerecht, wonach die Bilanz und die ihr zugrunde liegende Einnahme-Überschuss-

Rechnung in erster Linie auf die Feststellung der realisierten Gewinne und Verluste abstellt. Es gibt aber nicht realisierte Gewinne und Verluste, wie z.B. Wertsteigerungen des Anlagevermögens durch äußere Einflüsse, die durchaus einen bestimmenden Einfluss auf die Unternehmensbewertung haben können. Solche nicht von den Gesellschaftern veranlasste Wertänderungen werden in die gesonderte Erklärung über die gesamten Gewinne und Verluste aufgenommen, die entfallen kann, wenn derartige Effekte nicht auftreten.

Erklärung über Veränderungen bei der Bilanzierung

Wann immer ein Unternehmen seine Bilanzierungsgrundsätze gegenüber dem vorangegangenen Bilanzzeitraum verändert, ist dies zu erläutern. Hierzu dient die Erklärung über Veränderungen bei der Bilanzierung (note of historical profit or loss), die aber nur in diesem speziellen Fall abzugeben ist. Die kleine Limited im Auslandseinsatz wird in aller Regel ihre Bilanzierungsmethode in England nicht ändern - dazu besteht meist schon deshalb kein Anlass, weil in England in aller Regel kaum etwas zu versteuern ist, weshalb komplizierte Bilanzierungsmanöver in England die Ausnahme bleiben werden.

Bericht des Geschäftsführers

Zweck des schriftlichen Berichts des Geschäftsführers („Director's Report") ist die zusammenhängende, leicht lesbare und übersichtliche Zusammenfassung des finanziellen Status eines Unternehmens. Er enthält:

- Überblick über die Geschäftstätigkeit des Unternehmens im Berichtszeitraum
- Überblick über die Finanzentwicklung des Unternehmens im Berichtszeitraum
- Angaben über Geschäftsführergehälter
- Angaben zu den Mitarbeitern (Anzahl, Entwicklung)
- Spenden, Schenkungen
- ggf. Besonderheiten bei Prüfung und Steuern
- Geschäftsführungsstrukturen und Prinzipien (Corporate Governance)

Dieser Bericht ist bei kleinen Unternehmen entbehrlich.

Bericht des Wirtschaftsprüfers

Der Bericht des Wirtschaftsprüfers spielt bei kleinen Unternehmen keine Rolle und wird daher an dieser Stelle nicht behandelt.

ANLAGEN UND MUSTER

Einnahme-Überschuss-Rechnung: Zugelassene Formate

Muster 1

1. Turnover
2. Cost of sales
3. Gross profit or loss
4. Distribution costs
5. Administrative expenses
6. Other operating income
7. Income from shares in group undertakings
8. Income from participating interests
9. Income from other fixes asset investments
10. Other interest receivable and similar income
11. Amounts written off investments
12. Interst payable and similar charges
13. Tax on profit or loss on ordinary activities
14. Profit or loss on ordinary activities after taxation
    Minoritiy interests (group accounts only)
15. Extraordinary income
16. Extraordinary charges
17. Extraordinary profit or loss
18. Tax on extraordinary profit or loss
    Minoritiy interests (group accounts only)
19. Other taxes not shown under the above items
20. Profit or loss for the financial year

Muster 2

1. Turnover
2. Change in stocks of finished goods and work in progress
3. Own work capitalized
4. Other operating income
5. (a) Raw materials and consumables
   (b) Other external charges
6. Staff costs
   (a) wages and salaries
   (b) social security costs
   (c) other pension costs
7. (a) Depreciation and other amounts written off tangible and intangible fixed assets
   (b) Exeptional amounts written off current assets
8. Other operating charges
9. Income from shares in group undertakings
10. Income from participating interests
11. Income from other fixed asset investments
12. Other interest receivable and similar income
13. Amounts writen off investments
14. Interst payable and similar charges
15. Tax on profit or loss on ordinary activities
16. Profit or loss on ordinary activities after taxation
    Minority interests (Group accounts only)
17. Extraordinary income
18. Extraordinary charges
19. Extraordinary profit or loss
20. Tax on extraordinary profit or loss
    Minority interests (Group accounts only)
21. Other taxes not shown under the above items
22. Profit or loss for the financial year

Muster 3

A	Charges		B	Income
1	Cost of sales		1	Turnover
2	Distribution costs		2	Other operating income
3	Administrative expenses		3	Income from shares in group undertakings
4	Amounts written off investments		4	Income from participating interests
5	Interest payable and similar charges		5	Income from other fixed asset investments
6	Tax on profit or loss on ordinary activities		6	Other interest receivable and similar income
7	Profit or loss on ordinary activities after taxation Minority interests (Group accounts only)		7	Profit or loss on ordinary activities after taxation Minoritiy interests (Group accounts only)
8	Extraordinary charges		8	Extraordinary income
9	Tax on extraordinary profit or loss Minority interests (Group accounts only)			Minority interests (Group accounts only)
10	Other taxes not shown under the above items			
11	Profit or loss for the financial year		9	Profit or loss for the financial year

Muster 4

A	**Charges**	**B**	**Income**
1	Reduction in stocks of finished goods and in work in progress	1	Turnover
2	(a) Raw materials and consumables	2	Increase in stocks of finished goods and in work in progress
	(b) Other external charges	3	Own work capitalized
3	Staff costs	4	Other operating income
	(a) wages and salaries	5	Income from shares in group undertakings
	(b) social security costs	6	Income from participating interests
	(c) other pension costs	7	Income from other fixed assets investments
4	(a) Depreciation and other amounts written off tangible and intangible fixed assets	8	Other interest receivable and similar income
	(b) Exceptional amounts written off current assets	9	Profit or loss on ordinary activities after taxation
5	Other operating charges		Minority interests (Group accounts only)
6	Amounts written off investments	10	Extraordinary income (Group accounts only)
7	Interest payable and similar charges		Minority interests (Group accounts only)
8	Tax on profit or loss on ordinary activities	11	Profit or loss for the financial year
9	Profit or loss on ordinary activities after taxation		
10	Extraordinary charges		
11	Tax on extraordinary profit or loss Minority interests (Group accounts only)		
12	Other taxes not shown in the items above		
13	Profit or loss for the financial year		

Bilanz: Zugelassene Formate

Muster 1

A		**Called-up share capital not paid**
B		**Fixed assets**
	I	Intangible assets
	II	Tangible assets
	III	Investments
C		**Current assets**
	I	Stocks
	II	Deptors
	III	Investments
	IV	Cash at bank and in hand
D		**Prepayments and accrued income**
E		**Creditors: Amounts falling due within one year**
F		**Net current assets (liabilities)**
G		**Total assets less current liabilities**
H		**Creditors: Amounts falling due after more than one year**
I		**Provisions for liabilities and charges**
J		**Accruals and deffered income**
		Minority interests (Group accounts only)
K		**Capital and reserves**
	I	Called-up share capital
	II	Share premium account
	III	Revaluation reserve
	IV	Other reserves
	V	Profit and loss account
		Minority interests (Group accounts only)

Muster 2

	Assets		*Liabilities*
A	**Called-up share capital not paid**	**A**	**Capital and reserves**
		I	Called-up share capital
B	**Fixed assets**	II	Share premium account
I	Intangible assets	III	Revaluation reserve
II	Tangible assets	IV	Other reserves
III	Investments	V	Profit and loss account
			Minority interests (Group accounts only)
C	**Current assets**		
I	Stocks	**B**	**Provisions for liabilities and charges**
II	Debtors		
III	Investments	**C**	**Creditors**
IV	Cash at bank and in hand		
		D	**Accruals and deffered income**
D	**Prepayments and accrued income**		

Mustersatzung

Bei dem nachfolgenden Text handelt es sich um ein (recht ausführliches) Muster, das bezweckt, ein Gefühl dafür zu vermitteln, was ein Memorandum üblicherweise regelt[5]. Das Muster dient nicht dazu, in dieser Form ungeprüft übernommen zu werden. Hierzu muss man sich zuvor fachkundigen Rates versichern und es an die Besonderheiten des Einzelfalles anpassen.

THE COMPANIES ACT 1985

(AS AMENDED)

COMPANY LIMITED BY SHARES

MEMORANDUM OF ASSOCIATION

OF ....LIMITED

1. The Company's name is ....Limited

2. The Company's registered office is to be situated in England and Wales.

The Company's objects are:-

....

AND in furtherance of the said objects to do all or any of the following things: -

(a) To purchase, lease or otherwise acquire buildings or land or any estate or interest therein.

---

[5] entnommen aus: Degenhardt, die Limited in Deutschland, ISBN 3-937686-43-6

(b) Subject to such consents as are required by Law to sell, let on lease or tenancy, exchange, mortgage or otherwise dispose of buildings or land or any estate or interest therein.

(c) To repair, renovate, restore, rebuild, convert, alter and extend any building or land.

(d) To print and publish newspapers, newsletters, periodicals, books, leaflets or other publications.

(e) To represent, express and give effect to the views and opinions of members of the Company on all matters.

(f) To promote or oppose bills in parliament and other measures and to promote the views and aims of the Company to regulatory and statutory bodies.

(g) To organise and promote lectures and seminars and other means of providing education and training and all matters concerning the same.

(h) To co-operate with any local or public authority or other body concerned to achieve the object of the Company.

(i) Subject to Clause 4 hereof to enter into and carry out contracts and in particular to enter into agreements and engagements with administrators, researchers, lecturers, authors, producers, consultants and other persons and retain advisors and to reimburse such persons and advisers by salaries or fees.

(j) To co-operate with operators, manufacturers, dealers, traders, the press and other sources of publicity for the purpose of promoting the objects of the Company.

(k) To raise funds and to invite and receive contributions from any person or persons whatsoever by way of subscription, donation and otherwise provided that the Company shall not undertake any permanent trading activity in raising funds for its primary objects.

(l) Subject to such consents as may be required by law from time to time and subject as hereinafter provided, to borrow or raise money and to execute and issue security as the Company shall think fit including mortgages, charges or securities over the whole or any part of its assets, present or future, but only in connection with the day to day operational requirements of the Company.

(m) To draw, accept, endorse, issue or execute promissory notes, bills of exchange, bills of lading, warrants and other negotiable, transferable or mercantile instruments, for the purpose of or in connection with the objects of the company.

(n) To invest and deal with the moneys of the Company not immediately required in such manner as the Company may from time to time determine subject nevertheless to such conditions (if any) and such consents (if any) as may for the time being be imposed or required by law and subject also as hereinafter provided.

(o) Subject to Clause 4 hereof to employ and remunerate staff; to employ and remunerate agents; and to pay or provide pensions and similar benefits to the staff of the Company and their dependents.

(p) To make such charges as may be thought appropriate for any services provided by the Company.

(q) To pay out of funds of the Company the costs of forming and registering the Company.

(r) To do all such other lawful things as shall be considered incidental or conducive to or in furtherance of the attainment of the objects of the Company; and it is hereby declared that the generality of this present sub-clause shall not be prejudice or affected by any of the powers of the Company set out above.

4. The income and property of the Company whensoever derived shall be applied solely towards the promotion of the objects of the Company as set forth in this Memorandum of Association, and no portion thereof shall be paid or transferred directly, by way of dividend bonus or otherwise howsoever by way of profit, to the members of the Company.

PROVIDED that nothing herein shall prevent the payment in good faith of reasonable and proper remuneration to any officer or servant of the Company or to any member of the Company in return for any services actually rendered to the Company, nor prevent the payment of interest at a rate per annum not exceeding 2% less than the base lending rate prescribed by a clearing bank selected by the Council on money lent or reasonable and proper rent for premises demised or let by any member of the Company; but so that no member of the Council of Management or Governing Body shall be appointed to any salaried office of the Company or any office of the Company paid by fees, and that no remuneration or other benefit in money or money's worth shall be given by the Company to any member of such Council or Governing Body, except repayment of reasonable and proper out of pocket expenses and interest at the rate aforesaid on money lent or reasonable and proper rent for premises demised or let to the Company, provided that the provisions last aforesaid shall not apply to any payment to any Company of which a member of the Council of Management or Governing Body may be a member, and in which such member shall not hold more than one hundredth part of the capital, and such member shall not be bound to account for any share of profits he may receive in respect of any such payment.

5. The liability of the members is limited.

6. Every member of the Company undertakes to contribute to the assets of the Company in the event of the same being wound up while he is a member, or within one year after he ceases to be a member, for payments of the debts and liabilities of the Company contracted before he ceases to be a member, and of the costs, charges and expenses of winding up, and for the adjustment of the rights of the contributors among themselves, such and for the amount as may be required not exceeding One pound.

7. True accounts shall be kept of the sums of money received and expended by the Company and the matters in respect of which such receipts and expenditure take place, of all sales and purchases of property and goods by the Company and of the property, credits and liabilities of the Company, and subject to any reasonable restrictions as to the time and manner of inspecting the same that may be imposed in accordance with the regulations of the Company for the time being, such accounts shall be open to the inspection of the members. Once at least in every year the accounts of the Company shall be examined and the correctness of the income and expenditure account and balance sheet ascertained by one or more properly qualified Auditor or Auditors.

Auszüge aus dem Companies Act

Der Companies Act 1985 in der geltenden Fassung stellt das Rückgrat des englischen Gesellschaftsrechts dar. Wer immer eine „Limited" in Deutschland tatsächlich zu verwenden gedenkt, muss sich mit diesem Regelwerk vertraut machen. Es hat ähnlichen Charakter wie das deutsche Handelsgesetzbuch und das GmbH-Gesetz, unterscheidet sich inhaltlich jedoch zum Teil erheblich von den deutschen Regelungen.

Der Text gliedert sich in 23 Kapitel und umfasst annährend 800 Einzelparagraphen - dies allein zeigt die Komplexität des Regelwerks. Wir drucken hier lediglich die wesentlichen Vorschriften ab, die sich mit der Rechnungslegung befassen.

Part I: Company Accounts

Introduction

1. The provisions of this Part amend Part VII of the [1985 c. 6.] Companies Act 1985 (accounts and audit) by—

(a) inserting new provisions in place of sections 221 to 262 of that Act, and

(b) amending or replacing Schedules 4 to 10 to that Act and inserting new Schedules.

Provisions applying to companies generally

Accounting records

The following sections are inserted in Part VII of the [1985 c. 6.] Companies Act 1985 at the beginning of Chapter I (provisions applying to companies generally)—

"Accounting records

Duty to keep accounting records.

221.—(1) Every company shall keep accounting records which are sufficient to show and explain the company's transactions and are such as to—

(a) disclose with reasonable accuracy, at any time, the financial position of the company at that time, and

(b) enable the directors to ensure that any balance sheet and profit and loss account prepared under this Part complies with the requirements of this Act.

(2) The accounting records shall in particular con-

tain—

(a) entries from day to day of all sums of money received and expended by the company, and the matters in respect of which the receipt and expenditure takes place, and

(b) a record of the assets and <u>liabilities of the company</u>.

(3) If the company's business involves dealing in goods, the accounting records shall contain—

(a) statements of stock held by the company at the end of each financial year of the company,

(b) all statements of stocktakings from which any such statement of stock as is mentioned in paragraph (a) has been or is to be prepared, and

(c) except in the case of goods sold by way of ordinary retail trade, statements of all goods sold and purchased, showing the goods and the buyers and sellers in sufficient detail to enable all these to be identified.

(4) A parent company which has a subsidiary undertaking in relation to which the above requirements do not apply shall take reasonable steps to secure that the undertaking keeps such accounting records as to enable the directors of the parent company to ensure that any balance sheet and profit and loss account prepared under this Part complies with the requirements of this Act.

(5) If a company fails to comply with any provision of this section, every officer of the company who is in default is guilty of an offence unless he shows that he acted honestly and that in the circumstances in which the company's business was carried on the default was excusable.

(6) A person guilty of an offence under this section is liable to imprisonment or a fine, or both.

222.—(1) A company's accounting records shall be kept at its registered office or such other place as the directors think fit, and shall at all times be open to inspection by the company's officers.

Where and for how long records to be kept.

(2) If accounting records are kept at a place outside Great Britain, accounts and returns with respect to the business dealt with in the accounting records so kept shall be sent to, and kept at, a place in Great Britain, and shall at all times be open to such inspection.

(3) The accounts and returns to be sent to Great Britain shall be such as to—

(a) disclose with reasonable accuracy the financial position of the business in question at intervals of not more than six months, and

(b) enable the directors to ensure that the company's balance sheet and profit and loss account comply with the requirements of this Act.

(4) If a company fails to comply with any provision of subsections (1) to (3), every officer of the company who is in default is guilty of an offence, and liable to imprisonment or a fine or both, unless he shows that he acted honestly and that in the circumstances in which the company's business was carried on the default was excusable.

(5) Accounting records which a company is required by section 221 to keep shall be preserved by it—

(a) in the case of a private company, for three years from the date on which they are made, and

(b) in the case of a public company, for six years from the date on which they are made.

This is subject to any provision contained in rules made under section 411 of the Insolvency Act 1986 (company insolvency rules).

(6) An officer of a company is guilty of an offence, and liable to imprisonment or a fine or both, if he fails to take all reasonable steps for securing compliance by the company with subsection (5) or intentionally causes any default by the company under that subsection."

A company's financial year and accounting reference periods

The following sections are inserted in Part VII of the [1985 c. 66.] Companies Act 1985—

"A company's financial year and accounting reference periods A company's financial year.	A company's financial year and accounting reference periods
	223.—(1) A company's "financial year" is determined as follows
	(2) Its first financial year begins with the first day of its first accounting reference period and ends with the last day of that period or such other date, not more than seven days before or after the end of that period, as the directors may determine.
	(3) Subsequent financial years begin with the day immediately following the end of the company's previous financial year and end with the last day of its next accounting reference period or such other date, not more than seven days before or after the end of that period, as the directors may determine.
	(4) In relation to an undertaking which is not a company, references in this Act to its financial year are to any period in respect of which a profit and loss account of the undertaking is required to be made up (by its constitution or by the law under which it is established), whether that period is a year or not.

(5) The directors of a parent company shall secure that, except where in their opinion there are good reasons against it, the financial year of each of its subsidiary undertakings coincides with the company's own financial year.

Accounting reference periods and accounting reference date.	**224.**—(1) A company's accounting reference periods are determined according to its accounting reference date.

(2) A company may, at any time before the end of the period of nine months beginning with the date of its incorporation, by notice in the prescribed form given to the registrar specify its accounting reference date, that is, the date on which its accounting reference period ends in each calendar year.

(3) Failing such notice, a company's accounting reference date is—

(a) in the case of a company incorporated before the commencement of section 3 of the Companies Act 1989, 31st March;

(b) in the case of a company incorporated after the commencement of that section, the last day of the month in which the anniversary of its incorporation falls.

(4) A company's first accounting reference period is the period of more than six months, but not more than 18 months, beginning with the date of its incorporation and ending with its accounting reference date.

(5) Its subsequent accounting reference periods are successive periods of twelve months beginning immediately after the end of the previous accounting reference period and ending with its accounting reference date.

(6) This section has effect subject to the provisions of section 225 relating to the alteration of accounting refer-

ence dates and the consequences of such alteration.

Alteration of accounting reference date.

225.—(1) A company may by notice in the prescribed form given to the registrar specify a new accounting reference date having effect in relation to the company's current accounting reference period and subsequent periods.

(2) A company may by notice in the prescribed form given to the registrar specify a new accounting reference date having effect in relation to the company's previous accounting reference period and subsequent periods if—

(a) the company is a subsidiary undertaking or parent undertaking of another company and the new accounting reference date coincides with the accounting reference date of that other company, or

(b) an administration order under Part II of the Insolvency Act 1986 is in force.

A company's "previous accounting reference period" means that immediately preceding its current accounting reference period.

(3) The notice shall state whether the current or previous accounting reference period—

(a) is to be shortened, so as to come to an end on the first occasion on which the new accounting reference date falls or fell after the beginning of the period, or

(b) is to be extended, so as to come to an end on the second occasion on which that date falls or fell after the beginning of the period.

(4) A notice under subsection (1) stating that the current accounting reference period is to be extended is ineffective, except as mentioned below, if given less than five years after the end of an earlier accounting reference period of the company which was extended by virtue of this section.

This subsection does not apply—

(a) to a notice given by a company which is a subsidiary undertaking or parent undertaking of another company and the new accounting reference date coincides with that of the other company, or

(b) where an administration order is in force under Part II of the Insolvency Act 1986,

or where the Secretary of State directs that it should not apply, which he may do with respect to a notice which has been given or which may be given.

(5) A notice under subsection (2)(a) may not be given if the period allowed for laying and delivering accounts and reports in relation to the previous accounting reference period has already expired.

(6) An accounting reference period may not in any case, unless an administration order is in force under Part II of the Insolvency Act 1986, be extended so as to exceed 18 months and a notice under this section is ineffective if the current or previous accounting reference period as extended in accordance with the notice would exceed that limit."

Individual company accounts

—(1) The following section is inserted in Part VII of the [1985 c. 6.] Companies Act 1985—

Individual company accounts.

„Annual accounts

Duty to prepare in- **226.**—(1) The directors of every company shall prepare for each financial year of the company—

dividual company accounts.

(a) a balance sheet as at the last day of the year, and

(b) a profit and loss account.

Those accounts are referred to in this Part as the company's "individual accounts".

(2) The balance sheet shall give a true and fair view of the state of affairs of the company as at the end of the financial year; and the profit and loss account shall give a true and fair view of the profit or loss of the company for the financial year.

(3) A company's individual accounts shall comply with the provisions of Schedule 4 as to the form and content of the balance sheet and profit and loss account and additional information to be provided by way of notes to the accounts.

(4) Where compliance with the provisions of that Schedule, and the other provisions of this Act as to the matters to be included in a company's individual accounts or in notes to those accounts, would not be sufficient to give a true and fair view, the necessary additional information shall be given in the accounts or in a note to them.

(5) If in special circumstances compliance with any of those provisions is inconsistent with the requirement to give a true and fair view, the directors shall depart from that provision to the extent necessary to give a true and fair view.

Particulars of any such departure, the reasons for it and its effect shall be given in a note to the accounts.

"

(2) Schedule 4 to the [1978 c. 30.] Companies Act 1985 (form and content of company accounts) is amended in accordance with Schedule 1 to this Act.

Group accounts

—(1) The following section is inserted in Part VII of the [1986 c. 45.] Companies Act 1985—

"Duty to prepare group accounts.

Group accounts

227.—(1) If at the end of a financial year a company is a parent company the directors shall, as well as preparing individual accounts for the year, prepare group accounts.

(2) Group accounts shall be consolidated accounts comprising—

(a) a consolidated balance sheet dealing with the state of affairs of the parent company and its subsidiary undertakings, and

(b) a consolidated profit and loss account dealing with the profit or loss of the parent company and its subsidiary undertakings.

(3) The accounts shall give a true and fair view of the state of affairs as at the end of the financial year, and the profit or loss for the financial year, of the undertakings included in the consolidation as a whole, so far as concerns members of the company.

(4) A company's group accounts shall comply with the provisions of Schedule 4A as to the form and content of the consolidated balance sheet and consolidated profit and loss account and additional information to be provided by way of notes to the accounts.

(5) Where compliance with the provisions of that Schedule, and the other provisions of this Act, as to the matters to be included in a company's group accounts or in notes to those accounts, would not be sufficient to give a true and fair view, the necessary additional information shall be given in the accounts or in a note to them.

(6) If in special circumstances compliance with any of those provisions is inconsistent with the requirement to give a true and fair view, the directors shall depart from that provision to the extent necessary to give a true and fair view.

Particulars of any such departure, the reasons for it and its effect shall be given in a note to the accounts.

(2) Schedule 2 to this Act (form and content of group accounts) is inserted after Schedule 4 to the [1985 c. 6.] Companies Act 1985, as Schedule 4A.

(3) The following sections are inserted in Part VII of the [1985 c. 6.] Companies Act 1985—

"Exemption for parent companies included in accounts of larger group.

228.—(1) A company is exempt from the requirement to prepare group accounts if it is itself a subsidiary undertaking and its immediate parent undertaking is established under the law of a member State of the European Economic Community, in the following cases—

(a) where the company is a wholly-owned subsidiary of that parent undertaking;

(b) where that parent undertaking holds more than 50 per cent. of the shares in the company and notice requesting the preparation of group accounts has not been served on the company by shareholders holding in aggregate—

(i) more than half of the remaining shares in the company, or

(ii) 5 per cent. of the total shares in the company.

Such notice must be served not later than six months after the end of the financial year before that to which it relates.

(2) Exemption is conditional upon compliance with all of the following conditions—

(a) that the company is included in consolidated accounts for a larger group drawn up to the same date, or to an earlier date in the same financial year, by a parent undertaking established under the law of a member State of the European Economic Community;

(b) that those accounts are drawn up and audited, and that parent undertaking's annual report is drawn up, according to that law, in accordance with the provisions of the Seventh Directive (83/349/EEC);

(c) that the company discloses in its individual accounts that it is exempt from the obligation to prepare and deliver group accounts;

(d) that the company states in its individual accounts the name of the parent undertaking which draws up the group accounts referred to above and—

(i) if it is incorporated outside Great Britain, the country in which it is incorporated,

(ii) if it is incorporated in Great Britain, whether it is registered in England and Wales or in Scotland, and

(iii) if it is unincorporated, the address of its principal place of business;

(e) that the company delivers to the registrar, within the period allowed for delivering its individual accounts, copies of those group accounts and of the parent undertaking's annual report, together with the auditors' report on them; and

(f) that if any document comprised in accounts and reports delivered in accordance with paragraph (e) is in a language other than English, there is annexed to the copy of that document delivered a translation of it into English, certified in the prescribed manner to be a correct translation.

(3) The exemption does not apply to a company any of whose securities are listed on a stock exchange in any member State of the European Economic Commu-

nity.

(4) Shares held by directors of a company for the purpose of complying with any share qualification requirement shall be disregarded in determining for the purposes of subsection (1)(a) whether the company is a wholly-owned subsidiary.

(5) For the purposes of subsection (1)(b) shares held by a wholly-owned subsidiary of the parent undertaking, or held on behalf of the parent undertaking or a wholly-owned subsidiary, shall be attributed to the parent undertaking.

(6) In subsection (3) "securities" includes—

(a) shares and stock,

(b) debentures, including debenture stock, loan stock, bonds, certificates of deposit and other instruments creating or acknowledging indebtedness,

(c) warrants or other instruments entitling the holder to subscribe for securities falling within paragraph (a) or (b), and

(d) certificates or other instruments which confer—

(i) property rights in respect of a security falling within paragraph (a), (b) or (c),

(ii) any right to acquire, dispose of, underwrite or convert a security, being a right to which the holder would be entitled if he held any such security to which the certificate or other instrument relates, or

(iii) a contractual right (other than an option) to acquire any such security otherwise than by subscription.

Subsidiary undertakings

229.—(1) Subject to the exceptions authorised or required by this section, all the subsidiary undertakings of included in the consolidation.

the parent company shall be included in the consolidation.

(2) A subsidiary undertaking may be excluded from consolidation if its inclusion is not material for the purpose of giving a true and fair view; but two or more undertakings may be excluded only if they are not material taken together.

(3) In addition, a subsidiary undertaking may be excluded from consolidation where—

(a) severe long-term restrictions substantially hinder the exercise of the rights of the parent company over the assets or management of that undertaking, or

(b) the information necessary for the preparation of group accounts cannot be obtained without disproportionate expense or undue delay, or

(c) the interest of the parent company is held exclusively with a view to subsequent resale and the undertaking has not previously been included in consolidated group accounts prepared by the parent company.

The reference in paragraph (a) to the rights of the parent company and the reference in paragraph (c) to the interest of the parent company are, respectively, to rights and interests held by or attributed to the company for the purposes of section 258 (definition of "parent undertaking") in the absence of which it would not be the parent company.

(4) Where the activities of one or more subsidiary undertakings are so different from those of other undertakings to be included in the consolidation that their inclusion would be incompatible with the obligation to give a true and fair view, those undertakings shall be excluded from consolidation.

This subsection does not apply merely because some of the undertakings are industrial, some commercial and some provide services, or because they carry on industrial or commercial activities involving different products or provide different services.

(5) Where all the subsidiary undertakings of a parent company fall within the above exclusions, no group accounts are required."

(4) The following section is inserted in Part VII of the [1985 c. 6.] Companies Act 1985—

"Treatment of individual profit and loss account where group accounts prepared.

230.—(1) The following provisions apply with respect to the individual profit and loss account of a parent company where—

(a) the company is required to prepare and does prepare group accounts in accordance with this Act, and

(b) the notes to the company's individual balance sheet show the company's profit or loss for the financial year determined in accordance with this Act.

(2) The profit and loss account need not contain the information specified in paragraphs 52 to 57 of Schedule 4 (information supplementing the profit and loss account).

(3) The profit and loss account must be approved in accordance with section 233(1) (approval by board of directors) but may be omitted from the company's annual accounts for the purposes of the other provisions below in this Chapter.

(4) The exemption conferred by this section is conditional upon its being disclosed in the company's annual accounts that the exemption applies."

Additional disclosure required in notes to accounts

—(1) The following section is inserted in Part VII of the [1985 c. 6.] Companies Act 1985—

Additional disclosure required in notes to accounts

"Disclosure required in notes to accounts: related undertakings.

231.—(1) The information specified in Schedule 5 shall be given in notes to a company's annual accounts.

(2) Where the company is not required to prepare group accounts, the information specified in Part I of that Schedule shall be given; and where the company is required to prepare group accounts, the information specified in Part II of that Schedule shall be given.

(3) The information required by Schedule 5 need not be disclosed with respect to an undertaking which—

(a) is established under the law of a country outside the United Kingdom, or

(b) carries on business outside the United Kingdom,

if in the opinion of the directors of the company the disclosure would be seriously prejudicial to the business of that undertaking, or to the business of the company or any of its subsidiary undertakings, and the Secretary of State agrees that the information need not be disclosed.

This subsection does not apply in relation to the information required under paragraph 5(2), 6 or 20 of that Schedule.

(4) Where advantage is taken of subsection (3), that fact shall be stated in a note to the company's annual accounts.

(5) If the directors of the company are of the opinion that the number of undertakings in respect of which the company is required to disclose information under any provision of Schedule 5 to this Act is such that compliance with that provision would result in information of excessive length being given, the information need only be given in respect of—

(a) the undertakings whose results or financial position, in the opinion of the directors, principally affected the figures shown in the company's annual accounts, and

(b) undertakings excluded from consolidation under section 229(3) or (4).

This subsection does not apply in relation to the information required under paragraph 10 or 29 of that Schedule.

(6) If advantage is taken of subsection (5)—

(a) there shall be included in the notes to the company's annual accounts a statement that the information is given only with respect to such undertakings as are mentioned in that subsection, and

(b) the full information (both that which is disclosed in the notes to the accounts and that which is not) shall be annexed to the company's next annual return.

For this purpose the "next annual return" means that next delivered to the registrar after the accounts in question have been approved under section 233.

(7) If a company fails to comply with subsection (6)(b), the company and every officer of it who is in default is liable to a fine and, for continued contravention, to a daily default fine."

(2) Schedule 3 to this Act (disclosure of information: related undertakings) is substituted for Schedule 5 to the [1985 c. 6.] Companies Act 1985.

(3) The following section is inserted in Part VII of the [1985 c. 6.] Companies Act 1985—

"Disclosure required in notes to accounts: emoluments

232.—(1) The information specified in Schedule 6 shall be given in notes to a company's annual accounts.

(2) In that Schedule—

Part I relates to the emoluments of directors (including

and other benefits of directors and others.	emoluments waived), pensions of directors and past directors, compensation for loss of office to directors and past directors and sums paid to third parties in respect of directors' services,

Part II relates to loans, quasi-loans and other dealings in favour of directors and connected persons, and

Part III relates to transactions, arrangements and agreements made by the company or a subsidiary undertaking for officers of the company other than directors.

(3) It is the duty of any director of a company, and any person who is or has at any time in the preceding five years been an officer of the company, to give notice to the company of such matters relating to himself as may be necessary for the purposes of Part I of Schedule 6.

(4) A person who makes default in complying with subsection (3) commits an offence and is liable to a fine."

(4) Schedule 6 to the [1985 c. 6.] Companies Act 1985 is amended in accordance with Schedule 4 to this Act.

Approval and signing of accounts

The following section is inserted in Part VII of the [1985 c. 6.] Companies Act 1985—

"Approval and signing of accounts

Approval and signing of accounts.	**233.**—(1) A company's annual accounts shall be approved by the board of directors and signed on behalf of the board by a director of the company.

(2) The signature shall be on the company's balance sheet.

(3) Every copy of the balance sheet which is laid be-

fore the company in general meeting, or which is otherwise circulated, published or issued, shall state the name of the person who signed the balance sheet on behalf of the board.

(4) The copy of the company's balance sheet which is delivered to the registrar shall be signed on behalf of the board by a director of the company.

(5) If annual accounts are approved which do not comply with the requirements of this Act, every director of the company who is party to their approval and who knows that they do not comply or is reckless as to whether they comply is guilty of an offence and liable to a fine.

For this purpose every director of the company at the time the accounts are approved shall be taken to be a party to their approval unless he shows that he took all reasonable steps to prevent their being approved.

(6) If a copy of the balance sheet—

(a) is laid before the company, or otherwise circulated, published or issued, without the balance sheet having been signed as required by this section or without the required statement of the signatory's name being included, or

(b) is delivered to the registrar without being signed as required by this section,

the company and every officer of it who is in default is guilty of an offence and liable to a fine."

Directors' report

—(1) The following sections are inserted in Part VII of the [1985 c. 6.] Companies Act 1985—

"Directors' report

Duty to prepare directors' report.

234.—(1) The directors of a company shall for each financial year prepare a report—

(a) containing a fair review of the development of the business of the company and its subsidiary undertakings during the financial year and of their position at the end of it, and

(b) stating the amount (if any) which they recommend should be paid as dividend and the amount (if any) which they propose to carry to reserves.

(2) The report shall state the names of the persons who, at any time during the financial year, were directors of the company, and the principal activities of the company and its subsidiary undertakings in the course of the year and any significant change in those activities in the year.

(3) The report shall also comply with Schedule 7 as regards the disclosure of the matters mentioned there.

(4) In Schedule 7—

Part I relates to matters of a general nature, including changes in asset values, directors' shareholdings and other interests and contributions for political and charitable purposes,

Part II relates to the acquisition by a company of its own shares or a charge on them,

Part III relates to the employment, training and advancement of disabled persons,

Part IV relates to the health, safety and welfare at work of the company's employees, and

Part V relates to the involvement of employees in the affairs, policy and performance of the company.

(5) In the case of any failure to comply with the provisions of this Part as to the preparation of a directors' report and the contents of the report, every person who was a director of the company immediately before the end of the period for laying and delivering accounts and reports for the financial year in question is guilty of an offence and liable to a fine.

(6) In proceedings against a person for an offence under this section it is a defence for him to prove that he took all reasonable steps for securing compliance with the requirements in question.

Approval and signing of directors' report.

234A.—(1) The directors' report shall be approved by the board of directors and signed on behalf of the board by a director or the secretary of the company.

(2) Every copy of the directors' report which is laid before the company in general meeting, or which is otherwise circulated, published or issued, shall state the name of the person who signed it on behalf of the board.

(3) The copy of the directors' report which is delivered to the registrar shall be signed on behalf of the board by a director or the secretary of the company.

(4) If a copy of the directors' report—

(a) is laid before the company, or otherwise circulated, published or issued, without the report having been signed as required by this section or without the required statement of the signatory's name being included, or

(b) is delivered to the registrar without being signed as required by this section,

the company and every officer of it who is in default is guilty of an offence and liable to a fine."

(2) Schedule 7 to the [1985 c. 6.] Companies Act 1985 (matters to be in-

cluded in directors' report) is amended in accordance with Schedule 5 to this Act.

Auditors' report

The following sections are inserted in Part VII of the [1985 c. 6.] Companies Act 1985—

"Auditors' report

Auditors' report.

235.—(1) A company's auditors shall make a report to the company's members on all annual accounts of the company of which copies are to be laid before the company in general meeting during their tenure of office.

(2) The auditors' report shall state whether in the auditors' opinion the annual accounts have been properly prepared in accordance with this Act, and in particular whether a true and fair view is given—

(a) in the case of an individual balance sheet, of the state of affairs of the company as at the end of the financial year,

(b) in the case of an individual profit and loss account, of the profit or loss of the company for the financial year,

(c) in the case of group accounts, of the state of affairs as at the end of the financial year, and the profit or loss for the financial year, of the undertakings included in the consolidation as a whole, so far as concerns members of the company.

(3) The auditors shall consider whether the information given in the directors' report for the financial year for which the annual accounts are prepared is consistent with those accounts; and if they are of opinion that it is not they shall state that fact in their report.

Signature

236.—(1) The auditors' report shall state the names of

of auditors' report.

the auditors and be signed by them.

(2) Every copy of the auditors' report which is laid before the company in general meeting, or which is otherwise circulated, published or issued, shall state the names of the auditors.

(3) The copy of the auditors' report which is delivered to the registrar shall state the names of the auditors and be signed by them.

(4) If a copy of the auditors' report—

(a) is laid before the company, or otherwise circulated, published or issued, without the required statement of the auditors' names, or

(b) is delivered to the registrar without the required statement of the auditors' names or without being signed as required by this section,

the company and every officer of it who is in default is guilty of an offence and liable to a fine.

(5) References in this section to signature by the auditors are, where the office of auditor is held by a body corporate or partnership, to signature in the name of the body corporate or partnership by a person authorised to sign on its behalf.

Duties of auditors.

237.—(1) A company's auditors shall, in preparing their report, carry out such investigations as will enable them to form an opinion as to—

(a) whether proper accounting records have been kept by the company and proper returns adequate for their audit have been received from branches not visited by them, and

(b) whether the company's individual accounts are in

109

agreement with the accounting records and returns.

(2) If the auditors are of opinion that proper accounting records have not been kept, or that proper returns adequate for their audit have not been received from branches not visited by them, or if the company's individual accounts are not in agreement with the accounting records and returns, the auditors shall state that fact in their report.

(3) If the auditors fail to obtain all the information and explanations which, to the best of their knowledge and belief, are necessary for the purposes of their audit, they shall state that fact in their report.

(4) If the requirements of Schedule 6 (disclosure of information: emoluments and other benefits of directors and others) are not complied with in the annual accounts, the auditors shall include in their report, so far as they are reasonably able to do so, a statement giving the required particulars."

Publication of accounts and reports

The following sections are inserted in Part VII of the [1985 c. 6.] Companies Act 1985—

"Publication of accounts and reportsPersons entitled to receive copies of accounts and reports.

Publication of accounts and reports

238.—(1) A copy of the company's annual accounts, together with a copy of the directors' report for that financial year and of the auditors' report on those accounts, shall be sent to—

(a) every member of the company,

(b) every holder of the company's debentures, and

(c) every person who is entitled to receive notice of general meetings, not less than 21 days before the date of the meeting at which copies of those documents are to be laid in accordance with section 241.

(2) Copies need not be sent—

(a) to a person who is not entitled to receive notices of general meetings and of whose address the company is unaware, or

(b) to more than one of the joint holders of shares or debentures none of whom is entitled to receive such notices, or

(c) in the case of joint holders of shares or debentures some of whom are, and some not, entitled to receive such notices, to those who are not so entitled.

(3) In the case of a company not having a share capital, copies need not be sent to anyone who is not entitled to receive notices of general meetings of the company.

(4) If copies are sent less than 21 days before the date of the meeting, they shall, notwithstanding that fact, be deemed to have been duly sent if it is so agreed by all the members entitled to attend and vote at the meeting.

(5) If default is made in complying with this section, the company and every officer of it who is in default is guilty of an offence and liable to a fine.

(6) Where copies are sent out under this section over a period of days, references elsewhere in this Act to the day on which copies are sent out shall be construed as references to the last day of that period.

Right to de-   **239.**—(1) Any member of a company and any

mand copies of accounts and reports.	holder of a company's debentures is entitled to be furnished, on demand and without charge, with a copy of the company's last annual accounts and directors' report and a copy of the auditors' report on those accounts.

(2) The entitlement under this section is to a single copy of those documents, but that is in addition to any copy to which a person may be entitled under section 238.

(3) If a demand under this section is not complied with within seven days, the company and every officer of it who is in default is guilty of an offence and liable to a fine and, for continued contravention, to a daily default fine.

(4) If in proceedings for such an offence the issue arises whether a person had already been furnished with a copy of the relevant document under this section, it is for the defendant to prove that he had.

Requirements in connection with publication of accounts.	**240.**—(1) If a company publishes any of its statutory accounts, they must be accompanied by the relevant auditors' report under section 235.

(2) A company which is required to prepare group accounts for a financial year shall not publish its statutory individual accounts for that year without also publishing with them its statutory group accounts.

(3) If a company publishes non-statutory accounts, it shall publish with them a statement indicating—

(a) that they are not the company's statutory accounts,

(b) whether statutory accounts dealing with any financial year with which the non-statutory accounts purport to deal have been delivered to the registrar,

(c) whether the company's auditors have made a report under section 235 on the statutory accounts for any such financial year, and

(d) whether any report so made was qualified or contained a statement under section 237(2) or (3) (accounting records or returns inadequate, accounts not agreeing with records and returns or failure to obtain necessary information and explanations);

and it shall not publish with the non-statutory accounts any auditors' report under section 235.

(4) For the purposes of this section a company shall be regarded as publishing a document if it publishes, issues or circulates it or otherwise makes it available for public inspection in a manner calculated to invite members of the public generally, or any class of members of the public, to read it.

(5) References in this section to a company's statutory accounts are to its individual or group accounts for a financial year as required to be delivered to the registrar under section 242; and references to the publication by a company of "non-statutory accounts" are to the publication of—

(a) any balance sheet or profit and loss account relating to, or purporting to deal with, a financial year of the company, or

(b) an account in any form purporting to be a balance sheet or profit and loss account for the group consisting of the company and its subsidiary undertakings relating to, or purporting to deal with, a financial year of the company,

otherwise than as part of the company's statutory accounts.

(6) A company which contravenes any provision of this section, and any officer of it who is in default, is guilty of an offence and liable to a fine."

Laying and delivering of accounts and reports

The following sections are inserted in Part VII of the [1985 c. 6.] Companies Act 1985—

"Laying and delivering of accounts and reports

Accounts and reports to be laid before company in general meeting.	**241.**—(1) The directors of a company shall in respect of each financial year lay before the company in general meeting copies of the company's annual accounts, the directors' report and the auditors' report on those accounts. (2) If the requirements of subsection (1) are not complied with before the end of the period allowed for laying and delivering accounts and reports, every person who immediately before the end of that period was a director of the company is guilty of an offence and liable to a fine and, for continued contravention, to a daily default fine. (3) It is a defence for a person charged with such an offence to prove that he took all reasonable steps for securing that those requirements would be complied with before the end of that period. (4) It is not a defence to prove that the documents in question were not in fact prepared as required by this Part.
Accounts and reports to be delivered to the	**242.**—(1) The directors of a company shall in respect of each financial year deliver to the registrar a copy of the company's annual accounts together with a copy of the directors' report for that year and a copy of the audi-

registrar. tors' report on those accounts.

If any document comprised in those accounts or reports is in a language other than English, the directors shall annex to the copy of that document delivered a translation of it into English, certified in the prescribed manner to be a correct translation.

(2) If the requirements of subsection (1) are not complied with before the end of the period allowed for laying and delivering accounts and reports, every person who immediately before the end of that period was a director of the company is guilty of an offence and liable to a fine and, for continued contravention, to a daily default fine.

(3) Further, if the directors of the company fail to make good the default within 14 days after the service of a notice on them requiring compliance, the court may on the application of any member or creditor of the company or of the registrar, make an order directing the directors (or any of them) to make good the default within such time as may be specified in the order.

The court's order may provide that all costs of and incidental to the application shall be borne by the directors.

(4) It is a defence for a person charged with an offence under this section to prove that he took all reasonable steps for securing that the requirements of subsection (1) would be complied with before the end of the period allowed for laying and delivering accounts and reports.

(5) It is not a defence in any proceedings under this section to prove that the documents in question were not in fact prepared as required by this Part.

Civil penalty for failure to deliver ac- **242A.**—(1) Where the requirements of section 242(1) are not complied with before the end of the period allowed for laying and delivering accounts and reports, the counts. company is liable to a civil penalty.

This is in addition to any liability of the directors under section 242.

(2) The amount of the penalty is determined by reference to the length of the period between the end of the period allowed for laying and delivering accounts and reports and the day on which the requirements are complied with, and whether the company is a public or private company, as follows:—

Length of period	*Public company*	*Private company*
Not more than 3 months.	£500	£100
More than 3 months but not more than 6 months.	£1,000	£250
More than 6 months but not more than 12 months.	£2,000	£500
More than 12 months.	£5,000	£1,000

(3) The penalty may be recovered by the registrar and shall be paid by him into the Consolidated Fund.

(4) It is not a defence in proceedings under this section to prove that the documents in question were not in fact prepared as required by this Part.

Accounts of subsidiary undertakings to be appended in certain cases.

243.—(1) The following provisions apply where at the end of the financial year a parent company has as a subsidiary undertaking—

(a) a body corporate incorporated outside Great Britain which does not have an established place of business in Great Britain, or

(b) an unincorporated undertaking,

which is excluded from consolidation in accordance with section 229(4) (undertaking with activities different from the undertakings included in the consolidation).

(2) There shall be appended to the copy of the company's annual accounts delivered to the registrar in accordance with section 242 a copy of the undertaking's latest individual accounts and, if it is a parent undertaking, its latest group accounts.

If the accounts appended are required by law to be audited, a copy of the auditors' report shall also be appended.

(3) The accounts must be for a period ending not more than twelve months before the end of the financial year for which the parent company's accounts are made up.

(4) If any document required to be appended is in a language other than English, the directors shall annex to the copy of that document delivered a translation of it into English, certified in the prescribed manner to be a correct translation.

(5) The above requirements are subject to the following qualifications—

(a) an undertaking is not required to prepare for the purposes of this section accounts which would not otherwise be prepared, and if no accounts satisfying the above requirements are prepared none need be appended;

(b) a document need not be appended if it would not otherwise be required to be published, or made available for public inspection, anywhere in the world, but in that case the reason for not appending it shall be stated in a note to the company's accounts;

(c) where an undertaking and all its subsidiary undertakings are excluded from consolidation in accordance with section 229(4), the accounts of such of the subsidiary undertakings of that undertaking as are included in its consolidated group accounts need not be appended.

(6) Subsections (2) to (4) of section 242 (penalties, &c. in case of default) apply in relation to the requirements of this section as they apply in relation to the requirements of subsection (1) of that section.

Period allowed for laying and delivering accounts and reports.

244.—(1) The period allowed for laying and delivering accounts and reports is—

(a) for a private company, 10 months after the end of the relevant accounting reference period, and

(b) for a public company, 7 months after the end of that period.

This is subject to the following provisions of this section.

(2) If the relevant accounting reference period is the company's first and is a period of more than 12 months, the period allowed is—

(a) 10 months or 7 months, as the case may be, from the first anniversary of the incorporation of the company, or

(b) 3 months from the end of the accounting reference period,

whichever last expires.

(3) Where a company carries on business, or has interests, outside the United Kingdom, the Channel Islands and the Isle of Man, the directors may, in respect of any financial year, give to the registrar before the end of the period allowed by subsection (1) or (2) a notice in the prescribed form—

(a) stating that the company so carries on business or

has such interests, and

(b) claiming a 3 month extension of the period allowed for laying and delivering accounts and reports;

and upon such a notice being given the period is extended accordingly.

(4) If the relevant accounting period is treated as shortened by virtue of a notice given by the company under section 225 (alteration of accounting reference date), the period allowed for laying and delivering accounts is that applicable in accordance with the above provisions or 3 months from the date of the notice under that section, whichever last expires.

(5) If for any special reason the Secretary of State thinks fit he may, on an application made before the expiry of the period otherwise allowed, by notice in writing to a company extend that period by such further period as may be specified in the notice.

(6) In this section "the relevant accounting reference period" means the accounting reference period by reference to which the financial year for the accounts in question was determined."

Remedies for failure to comply with accounting requirements

The following sections are inserted in Part VII of the [1985 c. 6.] Companies Act 1985—

"Revision of defective accounts and reports- Voluntary revision of annual ac-	Remedies for failure to comply with accounting requirements

245.—(1) If it appears to the directors of a company that any annual accounts of the company, or any directors' report, did not comply with the requirements of this Act, they may prepare revised accounts or a revised report. |

119

counts or directors' report.

(2) Where copies of the previous accounts or report have been laid before the company in general meeting or delivered to the registrar, the revisions shall be confined to—

(a) the correction of those respects in which the previous accounts or report did not comply with the requirements of this Act, and

(b) the making of any necessary consequential alterations.

(3) The Secretary of State may make provision by regulations as to the application of the provisions of this Act in relation to revised annual accounts or a revised directors' report.

(4) The regulations may, in particular—

(a) make different provision according to whether the previous accounts or report are replaced or are supplemented by a document indicating the corrections to be made;

(b) make provision with respect to the functions of the company's auditors in relation to the revised accounts or report;

(c) require the directors to take such steps as may be specified in the regulations where the previous accounts or report have been—

(i) sent out to members and others under section 238(1),

(ii) laid before the company in general meeting, or

(iii) delivered to the registrar,

or where a summary financial statement based on the previous accounts or report has been sent to members under section 251;

(d) apply the provisions of this Act (including those creating criminal offences) subject to such additions, exceptions and modifications as are specified in the regulations.

(5) Regulations under this section shall be made by statutory instrument which shall be subject to annulment in pursuance of a resolution of either House of Parliament.

Secretary of State's notice in respect of annual accounts.

245A.—(1) Where copies of a company's annual accounts have been sent out under section 238, or a copy of a company's annual accounts has been laid before the company in general meeting or delivered to the registrar, and it appears to the Secretary of State that there is, or may be, a question whether the accounts comply with the requirements of this Act, he may give notice to the directors of the company indicating the respects in which it appears to him that such a question arises, or may arise.

(2) The notice shall specify a period of not less than one month for the directors to give him an explanation of the accounts or prepare revised accounts.

(3) If at the end of the specified period, or such longer period as he may allow, it appears to the Secretary of State that no satisfactory explanation of the accounts has been given and that the accounts have not been revised so as to comply with the requirements of this Act, he may if he thinks fit apply to the court.

(4) The provisions of this section apply equally to revised annual accounts, in which case the references to revised accounts shall be read as references to further revised accounts.

Application to court in respect of defective accounts.

245B.—(1) An application may be made to the court—

(a) by the Secretary of State, after having complied with section 245A, or

(b) by a person authorised by the Secretary of State for the purposes of this section, for a declaration or declarator that the annual accounts of a company do not comply with the requirements of this Act and for an order requiring the directors of the company to prepare revised accounts.

(2) Notice of the application, together with a general statement of the matters at issue in the proceedings, shall be given by the applicant to the registrar for registration.

(3) If the court orders the preparation of revised accounts, it may give directions with respect to—

(a) the auditing of the accounts,

(b) the revision of any directors' report or summary financial statement, and

(c) the taking of steps by the directors to bring the making of the order to the notice of persons likely to rely on the previous accounts,

and such other matters as the court thinks fit.

(4) If the court finds that the accounts did not comply with the requirements of this Act it may order that all or part of—

(a) the costs (or in Scotland expenses) of and incidental to the application, and

(b) any reasonable expenses incurred by the company in connection with or in consequence of the preparation of revised accounts,

shall be borne by such of the directors as were party to the approval of the defective accounts.

For this purpose every director of the company at the time the accounts were approved shall be taken to have been a party to their approval unless he shows that he took all reasonable steps to prevent their being approved.

(5) Where the court makes an order under subsection

(4) it shall have regard to whether the directors party to the approval of the defective accounts knew or ought to have known that the accounts did not comply with the requirements of this Act, and it may exclude one or more directors from the order or order the payment of different amounts by different directors.

(6) On the conclusion of proceedings on an application under this section, the applicant shall give to the registrar for registration an office copy of the court order or, as the case may be, notice that the application has failed or been withdrawn.

(7) The provisions of this section apply equally to revised annual accounts, in which case the references to revised accounts shall be read as references to further revised accounts.

Other persons authorised to apply to court.

245C.—(1) The Secretary of State may authorise for the purposes of section 245B any person appearing to him—

(a) to have an interest in, and to have satisfactory procedures directed to securing, compliance by companies with the accounting requirements of this Act,

(b) to have satisfactory procedures for receiving and investigating complaints about the annual accounts of companies, and

(c) otherwise to be a fit and proper person to be authorised.

(2) A person may be authorised generally or in respect of particular classes of case, and different persons may be authorised in respect of different classes of case.

(3) The Secretary of State may refuse to authorise a person if he considers that his authorisation is unnecessary having regard to the fact that there are one or more

123

other persons who have been or are likely to be authorised.

(4) Authorisation shall be by order made by statutory instrument which shall be subject to annulment in pursuance of a resolution of either House of Parliament.

(5) Where authorisation is revoked, the revoking order may make such provision as the Secretary of State thinks fit with respect to pending proceedings.

(6) Neither a person authorised under this section, nor any officer, servant or member of the governing body of such a person, shall be liable in damages for anything done or purporting to be done for the purposes of or in connection with—

(a) the taking of steps to discover whether there are grounds for an application to the court,

(b) the determination whether or not to make such an application, or

(c) the publication of its reasons for any such decision,

unless the act or omission is shown to have been in bad faith."

Exemptions and special provisions

Small and medium-sized companies and groups

—(1) The following sections are inserted in Part VII of the [1985 c. 6.] Companies Act 1985, as the beginning of a Chapter II—

Small and medium-sized companies and groups

Exemptions for small and me-

246.—(1) A company which qualifies as a small or medium-sized company in relation to a financial year—

(a) is exempt from the requirements of paragraph 36A of

dium-sized companies.

Schedule 4 (disclosure with respect to compliance with accounting standards), and

(b) is entitled to the exemptions provided by Schedule 8 with respect to the delivery to the registrar under section 242 of individual accounts and other documents for that financial year.

(2) In that Schedule—

Part I relates to small companies,

Part II relates to medium-sized companies, and

Part III contains supplementary provisions.

(3) A company is not entitled to the exemptions mentioned in subsection (1) if it is, or was at any time within the financial year to which the accounts relate—

(a) a public company,

(b) a banking or insurance company, or

(c) an authorised person under the Financial Services Act 1986,

or if it is or was at any time during that year a member of an ineligible group.

(4) A group is ineligible if any of its members is—

(a) a public company or a body corporate which (not being a company) has power under its constitution to offer its shares or debentures to the public and may lawfully exercise that power,

(b) an authorised institution under the Banking Act 1987,

(c) an insurance company to which Part II of the Insurance Companies Act 1982 applies, or

(d) an authorised person under the Financial Services Act 1986.

(5) A parent company shall not be treated as qualifying as a small company in relation to a financial year unless the group headed by it qualifies as a small group, and shall not be treated as qualifying as a medium-sized company in relation to a financial year unless that group qualifies as a medium-sized group (see section 249).

Qualification of company as small or medium-sized.

247.—(1) A company qualifies as small or medium-sized in relation to a financial year if the qualifying conditions are met—

(a) in the case of the company's first financial year, in that year, and

(b) in the case of any subsequent financial year, in that year and the preceding year.

(2) A company shall be treated as qualifying as small or medium-sized in relation to a financial year—

(a) if it so qualified in relation to the previous financial year under subsection (1); or

(b) if it was treated as so qualifying in relation to the previous year by virtue of paragraph (a) and the qualifying conditions are met in the year in question.

(3) The qualifying conditions are met by a company in a year in which it satisfies two or more of the following requirements—

Small company

1. Turnover	Not more than £2 million
2. Balance sheet total	Not more than £975,000
3. Number of employees	Not more than 50

Medium-sized company

| 1. Turnover | Not more than £8 million |

2. Balance sheet total	Not more than £3.9 million
3. Number of employees	Not more than 250.

(4) For a period which is a company's financial year but not in fact a year the maximum figures for turnover shall be proportionately adjusted.

(5) The balance sheet total means—

(a) where in the company's accounts Format 1 of the balance sheet formats set out in Part I of Schedule 4 is adopted, the aggregate of the amounts shown in the balance sheet under the headings corresponding to items A to D in that Format, and

(b) where Format 2 is adopted, the aggregate of the amounts shown under the general heading "Assets".

(6) The number of employees means the average number of persons employed by the company in the year (determined on a weekly basis).

That number shall be determined by applying the method of calculation prescribed by paragraph 56(2) and (3) of Schedule 4 for determining the corresponding number required to be stated in a note to the company's accounts.

(2) Schedule 6 to this Act is substituted for Schedule 8 to the [1985 c. 6.] Companies Act 1985.

(3) The following sections are inserted in Part VII of the [1985 c. 6.] Companies Act 1985—

"Exemption for small and medium-sized groups. **248.**—(1) A parent company need not prepare group accounts for a financial year in relation to which the group headed by that company qualifies as a small or medium-sized group and is not an ineligible group.

(2) A group is ineligible if any of its members is—

(a) a public company or a body corporate which (not being a company) has power under its constitution to offer its shares or debentures to the public and may lawfully exercise that power,

(b) an authorised institution under the Banking Act 1987,

(c) an insurance company to which Part II of the Insurance Companies Act 1982 applies, or

(d) an authorised person under the Financial Services Act 1986.

(3) If the directors of a company propose to take advantage of the exemption conferred by this section, it is the auditors' duty to provide them with a report stating whether in their opinion the company is entitled to the exemption.

(4) The exemption does not apply unless—

(a) the auditors' report states that in their opinion the company is so entitled, and

(b) that report is attached to the individual accounts of the company.

Qualification of group as small or medium-sized.

249.—(1) A group qualifies as small or medium-sized in relation to a financial year if the qualifying conditions are met—

(a) in the case of the parent company's first financial year, in that year, and

(b) in the case of any subsequent financial year, in that year and the preceding year.

(2) A group shall be treated as qualifying as small or medium-sized in relation to a financial year—

(a) if it so qualified in relation to the previous financial year under subsection (1); or

(b) if it was treated as so qualifying in relation to the previous year by virtue of paragraph (a) and the qualifying conditions are met in the year in question.

(3) The qualifying conditions are met by a group in a year in which it satisfies two or more of the following requirements—

Small group

1. Aggregate turnover	Not more than £2 million net (or £2.4 million gross)
2. Aggregate balance sheet total	Not more than £1 million net (or £1.2 million gross)
3. Aggregate number of employees	Not more than 50

Medium-sized group

1. Aggregate turnover	Not more than £8 million net (or £9.6 million gross)
2. Aggregate balance sheet total	Not more than £3.9 million net (or £4.7 million gross)
3. Aggregate number of employees	Not more than 250.

(4) The aggregate figures shall be ascertained by aggregating the relevant figures determined in accordance with section 247 for each member of the group.

In relation to the aggregate figures for turnover and balance sheet total, "net" means with the set-offs and other adjustments required by Schedule 4A in the case of group accounts and "gross" means without those set-offs and other adjustments; and a company may satisfy the relevant requirement on the basis of either the net or the gross figure.

(5) The figures for each subsidiary undertaking shall be those included in its accounts for the relevant financial year, that is—

(a) if its financial year ends with that of the parent company, that financial year, and

(b) if not, its financial year ending last before the end of the financial year of the parent company.

(6) If those figures cannot be obtained without disproportionate expense or undue delay, the latest available figures shall be taken."

Dormant companies

The following section is inserted in Part VII of the [1985 c. 6.] Companies Act 1985—

"Dormant companies

Resolution not to appoint auditors.

250.—(1) A company may by special resolution make itself exempt from the provisions of this Part relating to the audit of accounts in the following cases—

(a) if the company has been dormant from the time of its formation, by a special resolution passed before the first general meeting of the company at which annual accounts are laid;

(b) if the company has been dormant since the end of the previous financial year and—

(i) is entitled in respect of its individual accounts for that year to the exemptions conferred by section 246 on a small company, or would be so entitled but for being a member of an ineligible group, and

(ii) is not required to prepare group accounts for that

year, by a special resolution passed at a general meeting of the company at which the annual accounts for that year are laid.

(2) A company may not pass such a resolution if it is—

(a) a public company,

(b) a banking or insurance company, or

(c) an authorised person under the Financial Services Act 1986.

(3) A company is "dormant" during a period in which no significant accounting transaction occurs, that is, no transaction which is required by section 221 to be entered in the company's accounting records; and a company ceases to be dormant on the occurrence of such a transaction.

For this purpose there shall be disregarded any transaction arising from the taking of shares in the company by a subscriber to the memorandum in pursuance of an undertaking of his in the memorandum.

(4) Where a company is, at the end of a financial year, exempt by virtue of this section from the provisions of this Part relating to the audit of accounts—

(a) sections 238 and 239 (right to receive or demand copies of accounts and reports) have effect with the omission of references to the auditors' report;

(b) no copies of an auditors' report need be laid before the company in general meeting;

(c) no copy of an auditors' report need be delivered to the registrar, and if none is delivered, the copy of the balance sheet so delivered shall contain a statement by the directors, in a position immediately above the signature required by section 233(4), that the company was dormant throughout the financial year; and

(d) the company shall be treated as entitled in respect of its individual accounts for that year to the exemptions conferred by section 246 on a small company notwithstanding that it is a member of an ineligible group.

(5) Where a company which is exempt by virtue of this section from the provisions of this Part relating to the audit of accounts—

(a) ceases to be dormant, or

(b) would no longer qualify (for any other reason) to make itself exempt by passing a resolution under this section,

it shall thereupon cease to be so exempt.

Public listed companies: provision of summary financial statement

The following section is inserted in Part VII of the [1985 c. 6.] Companies Act 1985—

Public listed companies

Provision of summary financial statement to shareholders.

251.—(1) A public company whose shares, or any class of whose shares, are listed need not, in such cases as may be specified by regulations made by the Secretary of State, and provided any conditions so specified are complied with, send copies of the documents referred to in section 238(1) to members of the company, but may instead send them a summary financial statement.

In this subsection "listed" means admitted to the Official List of The International Stock Exchange of the United Kingdom and the Republic of Ireland Limited.

(2) Copies of the documents referred to in section

238(1) shall, however, be sent to any member of the company who wishes to receive them; and the Secretary of State may by regulations make provision as to the manner in which it is to be ascertained whether a member of the company wishes to receive them.

(3) The summary financial statement shall be derived from the company's annual accounts and the directors' report and shall be in such form and contain such information as may be specified by regulations made by the Secretary of State.

(4) Every summary financial statement shall—

(a) state that it is only a summary of information in the company's annual accounts and the directors' report;

(b) contain a statement by the company's auditors of their opinion as to whether the summary financial statement is consistent with those accounts and that report and complies with the requirements of this section and regulations made under it;

(c) state whether the auditors' report on the annual accounts was unqualified or qualified, and if it was qualified set out the report in full together with any further material needed to understand the qualification;

(d) state whether the auditors' report on the annual accounts contained a statement under—

(i) section 237(2) (accounting records or returns inadequate or accounts not agreeing with records and returns), or

(ii) section 237(3) (failure to obtain necessary information and explanations),

and if so, set out the statement in full.

(5) Regulations under this section shall be made by statutory instrument which shall be subject to annulment in pursuance of a resolution of either House of

Parliament.

(6) If default is made in complying with this section or regulations made under it, the company and every officer of it who is in default is guilty of an offence and liable to a fine.

(7) Section 240 (requirements in connection with publication of accounts) does not apply in relation to the provision to members of a company of a summary financial statement in accordance with this section."

Private companies: election to dispense with laying of accounts and reports before general meeting

The following sections are inserted in Part VII of the [1985 c. 6.] Companies Act 1985—

Private companies

Election to dispense with laying of accounts and reports before general meeting.

252.—(1) A private company may elect (by elective resolution in accordance with section 379A) to dispense with the laying of accounts and reports before the company in general meeting.

(2) An election has effect in relation to the accounts and reports in respect of the financial year in which the election is made and subsequent financial years.

(3) Whilst an election is in force, the references in the following provisions of this Act to the laying of accounts before the company in general meeting shall be read as references to the sending of copies of the accounts to members and others under section 238(1)—

(a) section 235(1) (accounts on which auditors are to report),

(b) section 270(3) and (4) (accounts by reference to

which distributions are justified), and

(c) section 320(2) (accounts relevant for determining company's net assets for purposes of ascertaining whether approval required for certain transactions);

and the requirement in section 271(4) that the auditors' statement under that provision be laid before the company in general meeting shall be read as a requirement that it be sent to members and others along with the copies of the accounts sent to them under section 238(1).

(4) If an election under this section ceases to have effect, section 241 applies in relation to the accounts and reports in respect of the financial year in which the election ceases to have effect and subsequent financial years.

Right of shareholder to require laying of accounts.

253.—(1) Where an election under section 252 is in force, the copies of the accounts and reports sent out in accordance with section 238(1)—

(a) shall be sent not less than 28 days before the end of the period allowed for laying and delivering accounts and reports, and

(b) shall be accompanied, in the case of a member of the company, by a notice informing him of his right to require the laying of the accounts and reports before a general meeting;

and section 238(5) (penalty for default) applies in relation to the above requirements as to the requirements contained in that section.

(2) Before the end of the period of 28 days beginning with the day on which the accounts and reports are sent out in accordance with section 238(1), any member or auditor of the company may by notice in writing deposited at the registered office of the company require that a

general meeting be held for the purpose of laying the accounts and reports before the company.

(3) If the directors do not within 21 days from the date of the deposit of such a notice proceed duly to convene a meeting, the person who deposited the notice may do so himself.

(4) A meeting so convened shall not be held more than three months from that date and shall be convened in the same manner, as nearly as possible, as that in which meetings are to be convened by directors.

(5) Where the directors do not duly convene a meeting, any reasonable expenses incurred by reason of that failure by the person who deposited the notice shall be made good to him by the company, and shall be recouped by the company out of any fees, or other remuneration in respect of their services, due or to become due to such of the directors as were in default.

(6) The directors shall be deemed not to have duly convened a meeting if they convene a meeting for a date more than 28 days after the date of the notice convening it."

Unlimited companies: exemption from requirement to deliver accounts and reports

The following section is inserted in Part VII of the [1985 c. 6.] Companies Act 1985—

Unlimited companies

Exemption from requirement to deliver

254.—(1) The directors of an unlimited company are not required to deliver accounts and reports to the registrar in respect of a financial year if the following conditions are met.

accounts and reports.

(2) The conditions are that at no time during the relevant accounting reference period—

(a) has the company been, to its knowledge, a subsidiary undertaking of an undertaking which was then limited, or

(b) have there been, to its knowledge, exercisable by or on behalf of two or more undertakings which were then limited, rights which if exercisable by one of them would have made the company a subsidiary undertaking of it, or

(c) has the company been a parent company of an undertaking which was then limited.

The references above to an undertaking being limited at a particular time are to an undertaking (under whatever law established) the liability of whose members is at that time limited.

(3) The exemption conferred by this section does not apply if at any time during the relevant accounting period the company carried on business as the promoter of a trading stamp scheme within the Trading Stamps Act 1964.

(4) Where a company is exempt by virtue of this section from the obligation to deliver accounts, section 240 (requirements in connection with publication of accounts) has effect with the following modifications—

(a) in subsection (3)(b) for the words from "whether statutory accounts" to "have been delivered to the registrar" substitute "that the company is exempt from the requirement to deliver statutory accounts", and

(b) in subsection (5) for "as required to be delivered to the registrar under section 242" substitute "as prepared in accordance with this Part and approved by the board of directors"."

Banking and insurance companies and groups: special provisions

—(1) The following sections are inserted in Part VII of the [1985 c. 6.] Companies Act 1985—

Banking and insurance companies and groups

Special provisions for banking and insurance companies.

255.—(1) A banking or insurance company may prepare its individual accounts in accordance with Part I of Schedule 9 rather than Schedule 4.

(2) Accounts so prepared shall contain a statement that they are prepared in accordance with the special provisions of this Part relating to banking companies or insurance companies, as the case may be.

(3) In relation to the preparation of individual accounts in accordance with the special provisions of this Part relating to banking or insurance companies, the references to the provisions of Schedule 4 in section 226(4) and (5) (relationship between specific requirements and duty to give true and fair view) shall be read as references to the provisions of Part I of Schedule 9.

(4) The Secretary of State may, on the application or with the consent of the directors of a company which prepares individual accounts in accordance with the special provisions of this Part relating to banking or insurance companies, modify in relation to the company any of the requirements of this Part for the purpose of adapting them to the circumstances of the company.

This does not affect the duty to give a true and fair view.

Special provisions for banking and insurance groups.

255A.—(1) The parent company of a banking or insurance group may prepare group accounts in accordance with the provisions of this Part as modified by Part II of Schedule 9.

(2) Accounts so prepared shall contain a statement

that they are prepared in accordance with the special provisions of this Part relating to banking groups or insurance groups, as the case may be.

(3) References in this Part to a banking group are to a group where—

(a) the parent company is a banking company, or

(b) at least one of the undertakings in the group is an authorised institution under the Banking Act 1987 and the predominant activities of the group are such as to make it inappropriate to prepare group accounts in accordance with the formats in Part I of Schedule 4.

(4) References in this Part to an insurance group are to a group where—

(a) the parent company is an insurance company, or

(b) the predominant activity of the group is insurance business and activities which are a direct extension of or ancillary to insurance business.

(5) In relation to the preparation of group accounts in accordance with the special provisions of this Part relating to banking or insurance groups, the references to the provisions of Schedule 4A in section 227(5) and (6) (relationship between specific requirements and duty to give true and fair view) shall be read as references to those provisions as modified by Part II of Schedule 9.

(6) The Secretary of State may, on the application or with the consent of the directors of a company which prepares group accounts in accordance with the special provisions of this Part relating to banking or insurance groups, modify in relation to the company any of the requirements of this Part for the purpose of adapting them to the circumstances of the company.

Modification   **255B.**—(1) In relation to a company which prepares

of disclosure requirements in relation to banking company or group.	accounts in accordance with the special provisions of this Part relating to banking companies or groups, the provisions of Schedule 5 (additional disclosure: related undertakings) have effect subject to Part III of Schedule 9. (2) In relation to a banking company, or the parent company of a banking company, the provisions of Schedule 6 (disclosure: emoluments and other benefits of directors and others) have effect subject to Part IV of Schedule 9.
Directors' report where accounts prepared in accordance with special provisions.	**255C.**—(1) The following provisions apply in relation to the directors' report of a company for a financial year in respect of which it prepares accounts in accordance with the special provisions of this Part relating to banking or insurance companies or groups. (2) The information required to be given by paragraph 6, 8 or 13 of Part I of Schedule 9 (which is allowed to be given in a statement or report annexed to the accounts), may be given in the directors' report instead. Information so given shall be treated for the purposes of audit as forming part of the accounts. (3) The reference in section 234(1)(b) to the amount proposed to be carried to reserves shall be construed as a reference to the amount proposed to be carried to reserves within the meaning of Part I of Schedule 9. (4) If the company takes advantage, in relation to its individual or group accounts, of the exemptions conferred by paragraph 27 or 28 of Part I of Schedule 9, paragraph 1 of Schedule 7 (disclosure of asset values) does not apply. (5) The directors' report shall, in addition to comply-

ing with Schedule 7, also comply with Schedule 10 (which specifies additional matters to be disclosed)."

(2) The following section is inserted in Part VII of the [1985 c. 6.] Companies Act 1985—

"Power to apply provisions to banking partnerships.

255D.—(1) The Secretary of State may by regulations apply to banking partnerships, subject to such exceptions, adaptations and modifications as he considers appropriate, the provisions of this Part applying to banking companies.

(2) A "banking partnership" means a partnership which is an authorised institution under the Banking Act 1987.

(3) Regulations under this section shall be made by statutory instrument.

(4) No regulations under this section shall be made unless a draft of the instrument containing the regulations has been laid before Parliament and approved by a resolution of each House."

(3) Schedule 9 to the [1985 c. 6.] Companies Act 1985 (form and content of special category accounts) is amended in accordance with Schedule 7 to this Act.

(4) In that Schedule—

Part I contains amendments relating to the form and content of accounts of banking and insurance companies and groups,

Part II contains provisions with respect to the group accounts of banking and insurance groups,

Part III contains provisions adapting the requirements of Schedule 5 to the [1985 c. 6.] Companies Act 1985 (additional disclosure: related undertakings), and

Part IV contains provisions relating to the requirements of Schedule 6 to that Act (additional disclosure: emoluments and other benefits of directors and others).

(5) Schedule 8 to this Act (directors' report where accounts prepared in accordance with special provisions for banking and insurance companies and groups) is substituted for Schedule 10 to the [1985 c. 6.] Companies Act 1985.

Supplementary provisions

Accounting standards

The following section is inserted in Part VII of the [1985 c. 6.] Companies Act 1985, as the beginning of a Chapter III—

Accounting standards

Accounting standards.

256.—(1) In this Part "accounting standards" means statements of standard accounting practice issued by such body or bodies as may be prescribed by regulations.

(2) References in this Part to accounting standards applicable to a company's annual accounts are to such standards as are, in accordance with their terms, relevant to the company's circumstances and to the accounts.

(3) The Secretary of State may make grants to or for the purposes of bodies concerned with—

(a) issuing accounting standards,

(b) overseeing and directing the issuing of such standards, or

(c) investigating departures from such standards or from the accounting requirements of this Act and taking steps to secure compliance with them.

(4) Regulations under this section may contain such

transitional and other supplementary and incidental provisions as appear to the Secretary of State to be appropriate.

Power to alter accounting requirements

The following section is inserted in Part VII of the [1985 c. 6.] Companies Act 1985—

"Power to alter accounting requirements

Power of Secretary of State to alter accounting requirements.

257.—(1) The Secretary of State may by regulations made by statutory instrument modify the provisions of this Part.

(2) Regulations which—

(a) add to the classes of documents required to be prepared, laid before the company in general meeting or delivered to the registrar,

(b) restrict the classes of company which have the benefit of any exemption, exception or special provision,

(c) require additional matter to be included in a document of any class, or

(d) otherwise render the requirements of this Part more onerous,

shall not be made unless a draft of the instrument containing the regulations has been laid before Parliament and approved by a resolution of each House.

(3) Otherwise, a statutory instrument containing regulations under this section shall be subject to annulment in pursuance of a resolution of either House of Parliament.

(4) Regulations under this section may—

(a) make different provision for different cases or classes of case,

(b) repeal and re-enact provisions with modifications of form or arrangement, whether or not they are modified in substance,

(c) make consequential amendments or repeals in other provisions of this Act, or in other enactments, and

(d) contain such transitional and other incidental and supplementary provisions as the Secretary of State thinks fit.

(5) Any modification by regulations under this section of section 258 or Schedule 10A (parent and subsidiary undertakings) does not apply for the purposes of enactments outside the Companies Acts unless the regulations so provide."

Parent and subsidiary undertakings

—(1) The following section is inserted in Part VII of the [1985 c. 6.] Companies Act 1985—

"Parent and subsidiary undertakings

Parent and subsidiary undertakings.

258.—(1) The expressions "parent undertaking" and "subsidiary undertaking" in this Part shall be construed as follows; and a "parent company" means a parent undertaking which is a company.

(2) An undertaking is a parent undertaking in relation to another undertaking, a subsidiary undertaking, if—

(a) it holds a majority of the voting rights in the undertaking, or

(b) it is a member of the undertaking and has the right

to appoint or remove a majority of its board of directors, or

(c) it has the right to exercise a dominant influence over the undertaking—

(i) by virtue of provisions contained in the undertaking's memorandum or articles, or

(ii) by virtue of a control contract, or

(d) it is a member of the undertaking and controls alone, pursuant to an agreement with other shareholders or members, a majority of the voting rights in the undertaking.

(3) For the purposes of subsection (2) an undertaking shall be treated as a member of another undertaking—

(a) if any of its subsidiary undertakings is a member of that undertaking, or

(b) if any shares in that other undertaking are held by a person acting on behalf of the undertaking or any of its subsidiary undertakings.

(4) An undertaking is also a parent undertaking in relation to another undertaking, a subsidiary undertaking, if it has a participating interest in the undertaking and—

(a) it actually exercises a dominant influence over it, or

(b) it and the subsidiary undertaking are managed on a unified basis.

(5) A parent undertaking shall be treated as the parent undertaking of undertakings in relation to which any of its subsidiary undertakings are, or are to be treated as, parent undertakings; and references to its subsidiary undertakings shall be construed accordingly.

(6) Schedule 10A contains provisions explaining expressions used in this section and otherwise supple-

menting this section."

(2) Schedule 9 to this Act (parent and subsidiary undertakings: supplementary provisions) is inserted after Schedule 10 to the [1985 c. 6.] Companies Act 1985, as Schedule 10A.

Other interpretation provisions

The following sections are inserted in Part VII of the [1985 c. 6.] Companies Act 1985—

Other interpretation provisions.

259.—(1) In this Part "undertaking" means—

(a) a body corporate or partnership, or

(b) an unincorporated association carrying on a trade or business, with or without a view to profit.

(2) In this Part references to shares—

(a) in relation to an undertaking with a share capital, are to allotted shares;

(b) in relation to an undertaking with capital but no share capital, are to rights to share in the capital of the undertaking; and

(c) in relation to an undertaking without capital, are to interests—

(i) conferring any right to share in the profits or liability to contribute to the losses of the undertaking, or

(ii) giving rise to an obligation to contribute to the debts or expenses of the undertaking in the event of a winding up.

(3) Other expressions appropriate to companies shall be construed, in relation to an undertaking which is not a company, as references to the corresponding persons, officers, documents or organs, as the case may be, appropriate to undertakings of that description.

This is subject to provision in any specific context providing for the translation of such expressions.

(4) References in this Part to "fellow subsidiary undertakings" are to un-

dertakings which are subsidiary undertakings of the same parent undertaking but are not parent undertakings or subsidiary undertakings of each other.

(5) In this Part "group undertaking", in relation to an undertaking, means an undertaking which is—

(a) a parent undertaking or subsidiary undertaking of that undertaking, or

(b) a subsidiary undertaking of any parent undertaking of that undertaking.

260.—(1) In this Part a "participating interest" means an interest held by an undertaking in the shares of another undertaking which it holds on a long-term basis for the purpose of securing a contribution to its activities by the exercise of control or influence arising from or related to that interest.

(2) A holding of 20 per cent. or more of the shares of an undertaking shall be presumed to be a participating interest unless the contrary is shown.

(3) The reference in subsection (1) to an interest in shares includes—

(a) an interest which is convertible into an interest in shares, and

(b) an option to acquire shares or any such interest;

and an interest or option falls within paragraph (a) or (b) notwithstanding that the shares to which it relates are, until the conversion or the exercise of the option, unissued.

(4) For the purposes of this section an interest held on behalf of an undertaking shall be treated as held by it.

(5) For the purposes of this section as it applies in relation to the expression "participating interest" in section 258(4) (definition of "subsidiary undertaking")—

(a) there shall be attributed to an undertaking any interests held by any of its subsidiary undertakings, and

(b) the references in subsection (1) to the purpose and activities of an undertaking include the purposes and activities of any of its subsidiary undertakings and of the group as a whole.

(6) In the balance sheet and profit and loss formats set out in Part I of

147

Schedule 4, "participating interest" does not include an interest in a group undertaking.

(7) For the purposes of this section as it applies in relation to the expression "participating interest"—

(a) in those formats as they apply in relation to group accounts, and

(b) in paragraph 20 of Schedule 4A (group accounts: undertakings to be accounted for as associated undertakings),

the references in subsections (1) to (4) to the interest held by, and the purposes and activities of, the undertaking concerned shall be construed as references to the interest held by, and the purposes and activities of, the group (within the meaning of paragraph 1 of that Schedule).

261.—(1) Information required by this Part to be given in notes to a company's annual accounts may be contained in the accounts or in a separate document annexed to the accounts. (2) References in this Part to a company's annual accounts, or to a balance sheet or profit and loss account, include notes to the accounts giving information which is required by any provision of this Act, and required or allowed by any such provision to be given in a note to company accounts.

262.—(1) In this Part—

"annual accounts" means—

(a) the individual accounts required by section 226, and

(b) any group accounts required by section 227,

(but see also section 230 (treatment of individual profit and loss account where group accounts prepared));

"annual report", in relation to a company, means the directors' report required by section 234;

"balance sheet date" means the date as at which the balance sheet was made up;

"capitalisation", in relation to work or costs, means treating that work or those costs as a fixed asset;

"credit institution" means an undertaking carrying on a deposit-taking business within the meaning of the Banking Act 1987;

"fixed assets" means assets of a company which are intended for use on a continuing basis in the company's activities, and "current assets" means assets not intended for such use;

"group" means a parent undertaking and its subsidiary undertakings;

"included in the consolidation", in relation to group accounts, or "included in consolidated group accounts", means that the undertaking is included in the accounts by the method of full (and not proportional) consolidation, and references to an undertaking excluded from consolidation shall be construed accordingly;

"purchase price", in relation to an asset of a company or any raw materials or consumables used in the production of such an asset, includes any consideration (whether in cash or otherwise) given by the company in respect of that asset or those materials or consumables, as the case may be;

"qualified", in relation to an auditors' report, means that the report does not state the auditors' unqualified opinion that the accounts have been properly prepared in accordance with this Act or, in the case of an undertaking not required to prepare accounts in accordance with this Act, under any corresponding legislation under which it is required to prepare accounts;

"true and fair view" refers—

(a) in the case of individual accounts, to the requirement of section 226(2), and

(b) in the case of group accounts, to the requirement of section 227(3);

"turnover", in relation to a company, means the amounts derived from the provision of goods and services falling within the company's ordinary activities, after deduction of—

(i) trade discounts,

(ii) value added tax, and

(iii) any other taxes based on the amounts so derived.

(2) In the case of an undertaking not trading for profit, any reference in this Part to a profit and loss account is to an income and expenditure account;

and references to profit and loss and, in relation to group accounts, to a consolidated profit and loss account shall be construed accordingly.

(3) References in this Part to "realised profits" and "realised losses", in relation to a company's accounts, are to such profits or losses of the company as fall to be treated as realised in accordance with principles generally accepted, at the time when the accounts are prepared, with respect to the determination for accounting purposes of realised profits or losses.

This is without prejudice to—

(a) the construction of any other expression (where appropriate) by reference to accepted accounting principles or practice, or

(b) any specific provision for the treatment of profits or losses of any description as realised.

262A. The following Table shows the provisions of this Part defining or otherwise explaining expressions used in this Part (other than expressions used only in the same section or paragraph)—

"

accounting reference date and accounting reference period	section 224
accounting standards and applicable accounting standards	section 256
annual accounts	
(generally)	section 262(1)
(includes notes to the accounts)	section 261(2)
annual report	section 262(1)
associated undertaking (in Schedule 4A)	paragraph 20 of that Schedule

balance sheet (includes notes)	section 261(2)
balance sheet date	section 262(1)
banking group	section 255A(3)
capitalisation (in relation to work or costs)	section 262(1)
credit institution	section 262(1)
current assets	section 262(1)
fellow subsidiary undertaking	section 259(4)
financial year	section 223
fixed assets	section 262(1)
group	section 262(1)
group undertaking	section 259(5)
historical cost accounting rules (in Schedule 4)	paragraph 29 of that Schedule
included in the consolidation and related expressions	section 262(1)
individual accounts	section 262(1)
insurance group	section 255A(4)
land of freehold tenure and land of leasehold tenure (in relation to Scotland)	
—in Schedule 4	paragraph 93 of that Schedule

—in Schedule 9	paragraph 36 of that Schedule
lease, long lease and short lease	
—in Schedule 4	paragraph 83 of that Schedule
—in Schedule 9	paragraph 34 of that Schedule
listed investment	
—in Schedule 4	paragraph 84 of that Schedule
—in Schedule 9	paragraph 33 of that Schedule
notes to the accounts	section 261(1)
parent undertaking (and parent company)	section 258 and Schedule 10A
participating interest	section 260
pension costs (in Schedule 4)	paragraph 94(2) and (3) of that Schedule
period allowed for laying and delivering accounts and reports	section 244
profit and loss account	
(includes notes)	section 261(2)
(in relation to a company not trading for profit)	section 262(2)

provision	
—in Schedule 4	paragraphs 88 and 89 of that Schedule
—in Schedule 9	paragraph 32 of that Schedule
purchase price	section 262(1)
qualified	section 262(1)
realised losses and realised profits	section 262(3)
reserve (in Schedule 9)	paragraph 32 of that Schedule
shares	section 259(2)
social security costs (in Schedule 4)	paragraph 94(1) and (3) of that Schedule
special provisions for banking and insurance companies and groups	sections 255 and 255A
subsidiary undertaking	section 258 and Schedule 10A
true and fair view	section 262(1)
turnover	section 262(1)
undertaking and related expressions	section 259(1) to (3)

"

Consequential amendments

Consequential amendments

The enactments specified in Schedule 10 have effect with the amendments specified there, which are consequential on the amendments made by the preceding provisions of this Part.

Anhang 1 zum Companies Act (Form and Content of Company Accounts)

SCHEDULE 1

Section 4(2).

Form and Content of Company Accounts

1. Schedule 4 to the [1985 c. 6.] Companies Act 1985 (form and content of company accounts) is amended as follows.

Group undertakings

2.—(1) For "group companies", wherever occurring, substitute "group undertakings".

(2) That expression occurs—

    (a) in Balance Sheet Format 1, in Items B.III.1 and 2, C.II.2, C.III.1, E.6 and H.6;

    (b) in Balance Sheet Format 2—

        (i) under the heading "ASSETS", in Items B.III.1 and 2, C.II.2 and C.III.1;

        (ii) under the heading "LIABILITIES", in Item C.6;

    (c) in the Profit and Loss Accounts Formats—

        (i) in Format 1, Item 7;

(ii) in Format 2, Item 9;

(iii) in Format 3, Item B.3;

(iv) in Format 4, Item B.5;

(d) in Notes (15) and (16) to the profit and loss account formats; and

(e) in the second sentence of paragraph 53(2) (exclusion from requirement to state separately certain loans).

Participating interests

3.—(1) For "shares in related companies", wherever occurring, substitute "participating interests".

(2) That expression occurs—

(a) in Balance Sheet Format 1, Item B.III.3;

(b) in Balance Sheet Format 2, under the heading "ASSETS", in Item B.III.3;

(c) in the Profit and Loss Accounts Formats—

(i) in Format 1, Item 8;

(ii) in Format 2, Item 10;

(iii) in Format 3, Item B.4;

(iv) in Format 4, Item B.6.

4.—(1) For "related companies", wherever occurring in any other context, substitute "undertakings in which the company has a participating interest".

(2) Those contexts are—

(a) in Balance Sheet Format 1, in Items B.III.4, C.II.3, E.7 and H.7;

(b) in Balance Sheet Format 2—

(i) under the heading "ASSETS", in Items B.III.4 and C.II.3;

(ii) under the heading "LIABILITIES", in Item C.7.

Consistency of accounting policies

5. For paragraph 11 (consistency of accounting policy from one year to the next) substitute—

"**11.** Accounting policies shall be applied consistently within the same accounts and from one financial year to the next.".

Revaluation reserve

6. In paragraph 34 (revaluation reserve), for sub-paragraph (3) (circumstances in which reduction of reserve required or permitted) substitute—

"(3) An amount may be transferred from the revaluation reserve—

(a) to the profit and loss account, if the amount was previously charged to that account or represents realised profit, or

(b) on capitalisation;

and the revaluation reserve shall be reduced to the extent that the amounts transferred to it are no longer necessary for the purposes of the valuation method used.

(3A) In sub-paragraph (3)(b) "capitalisation", in relation to an amount standing to the credit of the revaluation reserve, means applying it in wholly or partly paying up unissued shares in the company to be allotted to members of the company as fully or partly paid shares.

(3B) The revaluation reserve shall not be reduced except as mentioned in this paragraph." .

Compliance with accounting standards

7. After paragraph 36 (disclosure of accounting policies) insert—

"**36A.** It shall be stated whether the accounts have been prepared in accordance with applicable accounting standards and particulars of any material departure from those standards and the reasons for it shall be given." .

Provision for taxation

8. For paragraph 47 (provision for taxation) substitute—

"**47.** The amount of any provision for deferred taxation shall be stated separately from the amount of any provision for other taxation." .

Loans in connection with assistance for purchase of company's own shares

9. In paragraph 51(2) (disclosure of outstanding loans in connection with certain cases of financial assistance for pur-

chase of company's own shares), after "153(4)(b)" insert ", (bb)".

Obligation to show corresponding amounts for previous financial year

10. In paragraph 58(3) (exceptions from obligation to show corresponding amount for previous financial year), for paragraphs (a) to (c) substitute—

"(a) paragraph 13 of Schedule 4A (details of accounting treatment of acquisitions),

(b) paragraphs 2, 8(3), 16, 21(1)(d), 22(4) and (5), 24(3) and (4) and 27(3) and (4) of Schedule 5 (shareholdings in other undertakings),

(c) Parts II and III of Schedule 6 (loans and other dealings in favour of directors and others), and

(d) paragraphs 42 and 46 above (fixed assets and reserves and provisions)." .

Special provisions where company is parent company or subsidiary undertaking

11.—(1) For the heading to Part IV (special provisions where the company is a holding or subsidiary company) substitute—

"Part IV

Special Provisions Where Company is a Parent Company or Subsidiary Undertaking

(2) In that Part for paragraph 59 substitute—

"Dealings with or interests in group undertakings

59. Where a company is a parent company or a subsidiary undertaking and any item required by Part I of this Schedule to be shown in the company's balance sheet in relation to group undertakings includes—

(a) amounts attributable to dealings with or interests in any parent undertaking or fellow subsidiary undertaking, or

(b) amounts attributable to dealings with or interests in any subsidiary undertaking of the company,

the aggregate amounts within paragraphs (a) and (b) respectively shall be shown as separate items, either by way of subdivision of the relevant item in the balance sheet or in a note to the company's accounts.

(3) After that paragraph insert—

"Guarantees and other financial commitments in favour of group undertakings

59A. Commitments within any of sub-paragraphs (1) to (5) of paragraph 50 (guarantees and other financial commitments) which are undertaken on behalf of or for the benefit of—

(a) any parent undertaking or fellow

subsidiary undertaking, or

(b) any subsidiary undertaking of the company,

shall be stated separately from the other commitments within that sub-paragraph, and commitments within paragraph (a) shall also be stated separately from those within paragraph (b).